CATHARSIS

Penang Institute, one of Malaysia's major think tanks, is funded by the Penang State Government. Established in 1997 as SERI, it underwent a name change in 2011 as part of a rebranding exercise carried out to reflect heightened ambitions to secure Penang's reputation as an intellectual hub and as the culture capital of the country, and to enhance its understanding of ASEAN and beyond.

With the tagline 'Making Ideas Work', Penang Institute encourages bold and innovative thinking not only in academic disciplines, but also through supporting literature by way of events such as book launches and public literature seminars; participation in the annual George Town Literary Festival; and through its renowned magazine *Penang Monthly*. Its policy brief, *ISSUES*, was launched in June 2017, and its *Penang Institute Podcasts* series in August 2018.

❖   ❖   ❖

The **ISEAS – Yusof Ishak Institute** (formerly Institute of Southeast Asian Studies) is an autonomous organization established in 1968. It is a regional centre dedicated to the study of socio-political, security, and economic trends and developments in Southeast Asia and its wider geostrategic and economic environment. The Institute's research programmes are grouped under Regional Economic Studies (RES), Regional Strategic and Political Studies (RSPS), and Regional Social and Cultural Studies (RSCS). The Institute is also home to the ASEAN Studies Centre (ASC), the Nalanda-Sriwijaya Centre (NSC), and the Singapore APEC Study Centre.

ISEAS Publishing, an established academic press, has issued more than 2,000 books and journals. It is the largest scholarly publisher of research about Southeast Asia from within the region. ISEAS Publishing works with many other academic and trade publishers and distributors to disseminate important research and analyses from and about Southeast Asia to the rest of the world.

❖   ❖   ❖

The **Strategic Information and Research Development Centre (SIRD)** is an independent publishing house founded in January 2000 in Petaling Jaya, Malaysia. The SIRD list focuses on Malaysian and Southeast Asian studies, economics, gender studies, social sciences, politics and international relations. Our books address the scholarly community, students, the NGO and development communities, policymakers, activists and the wider public. SIRD also distributes titles (via its sister organisation, **GB Gerakbudaya Enterprise Sdn Bhd**) published by scholarly and institutional presses, NGOs and other independent publishers. We also organise seminars, forums and group discussions. All this, we believe, is conducive to the development and consolidation of the notions of civil liberty and democracy.

CATHARSIS

A Second Chance for
Democracy in Malaysia

Ooi Kee Beng

PENANG
INSTITUTE
making ideas work

SIRD

ISEAS
YUSOF ISHAK
INSTITUTE

Copyright © 2018 Ooi Kee Beng

First published in 2018 by
Strategic Information and Research Development Centre
No. 2 Jalan Bukit 11/2, 46200 Petaling Jaya, Selangor, Malaysia
Email: gerak@gerakbudaya.com
Website: www.gerakbudaya.com

and

Penang Institute
10 Brown Road, 10350 Penang, Malaysia
Email: enquiry@penanginstitute.org
Website: www.penanginstitute.org

Co-published in Singapore in 2018 by ISEAS Publishing
ISEAS - Yusof Ishak Institute, 30 Heng Mui Keng Terrace, Singapore 119614
Email: publish@iseas.edu.sg
Website: bookshop.iseas.edu.sg

Perpustakaan Negara Malaysia / Cataloguing-in-Publication Data

Ooi, Kee Beng, 1955-
    Catharsis: A Second Chance for Democracy in Malaysia / Ooi Kee Beng.
    ISBN 978-967-2165-31-6
    1. Malaysia–Politics and government.
    2. Malaysia–Social conditions. 1. Title.
    320.9595

ISEAS Library / Cataloguing-in-Publication Data

Ooi, Kee Beng, 1955-
Catharsis : A Second Chance for Democracy in Malaysia.
1. Malaysia—Politics and government—21 st century.
2. Political culture—Malaysia.
3. Democracy—Malaysia.
I. Title.
DS597.2 O591 2018

ISBN 978-981-4818-91-9 (soft cover)
ISBN 978-981-4818-92-6 (e-book, PDF)

Copy-editing by Kim Khaira
Cover design and layout by Janice Cheong

Printed by Vinlin Press Sdn Bhd
2 Jalan Meranti Permai 1
Meranti Permai Industrial Park
Batu 15, Jalan Puchong
47100 Puchong, Selangor, Malaysia

Contents

Foreword by Liew Chin Tong   ix

1. Introduction – Malaysia's Future Is Redeemed   1

Before Pakatan Harapan

2. After All These Years, Malaysia Is Still Held Hostage   7
3. Beyond the Nationalism Trap   10
4. Federating Malaysia — A Continuous and Troubled Process   13
5. Funeral for a True Son of Penang   16
6. Let's Work Out What Malaysia Is Good For   18
7. The Unity Fetish   21
8. When the National Narrative Loses the Script   28
9. Let's Be Cosmopolitan and Leave Multi-ethnicity Behind   32
10. Noses Don't Grow Back   34
11. Mahathir's Bersatu is Best Understood as an NGO   37

Before 9 May 2018

12. Racialising the Un-racialisable: What Is the Red Shirt Rally All About?   41
13. One Country's Merdeka Is Another's Damage Control   44
14. Malaysia – Where Politics Must Be Ethnically Inclusive and Exclusive at the Same Time   48
15. Is Malaysia at a Crossroads or in a Quagmire?   52
16. Unity Without Solidarity Sows Disunity   55
17. UMNO and Looking Back at History   58
18. Sarawak Forces Federal Opposition to Do Deep Soul-searching. But Can It?   61
19. By-elections Reveal New Malay Politics   64

20. Interview with Mahathir Mohamad: 'People Must Be Able to Hold Their Heads Up.' 68
21. Malaysia Has to Start Re-examining Its Histories 75
22. Waves from US Probe into 1MDB May Turn into Tsunami 79
23. Seeking a New Formula to Unite Malaysia's Diversity 82
24. Time for Anwar to Accept Mahathir's Olive Branch? 85
25. Najib, Mahathir and the Timing of Malaysia's Polls 88
26. Excessive Governance Is Not Good Governance 92
27. Why Malaysia's Opposition Will Take to the Streets Again 95
28. Merdeka is About The Individual, Too 99
29. A Battle Between Malay Leaders Over Malaysia's Future 102
30. The Primacy of Political Economy in Asia 105

With Mahathir at the Helm

31. One Thing Is Certain—There Will Be More Amendments to the Constitution 111
32. The More Things Change, the More Things May Actually Change 114
33. Did Merdeka Liberate or Create Malaya? 119
34. Interview with Nurul Izzah Anwar: Rebuilding a Nation Long Divided 122
35. The Diminishing of Humans Through Identity Politics 133
36. The Art of Dismantling Cultural Pluralism 136
37. No Need to Let Bigots Dictate Policy 141
38. What the Penang Floods Say About Malaysian Politics (and It's Not Just About Climate Change) 145
39. This is the Moment of Truth for Malaysia's Race-based Politics 149
40. We are Equal Only Through Our Vote 153
41. Why the Opposition Has a Shot at Toppling the Barisan Nasional with Mahathir at the Helm 156
42. Spiralling Back towards Reformasi 160
43. Individual Freedom Is a Matter of National Survival 163
44. Why Meet the Twenty-first Century with Twentieth Century Mindsets? 166
45. A Final Quarrel between a Repentant Grandfather and Old-fashioned Self-absorbed Parents 169
46. Outraged Enough to Go Vote or Cynical Enough to Stay Home? 172

Beyond 9 May 2018

47. The Bewildering Game of Malaysian Politics, the Rot Within the
    Barisan Nasional 183
48. A Revolution in Malaysia? Not So Fast... 187
49. Mahathir: Renaissance Man 191
50. Malaysia's Reformasi Movement Lives Up To Its Name 194
51. In Lieu of Race and Religion 201
52. It All Seems So Simple Now... 205
53. Catharsis – The Rebirth of Malaysia Finally Begins 208
54. A Malaysian Spring for Intelligentsia? 215
55. The Layers of Historical Significance of GE14 218

About the Author 222

Foreword

by Liew Chin Tong

Reading Ooi Kee Beng's *Catharsis* a month or so after the historic 9 May 2018 general election has been such a joy. These pages essentially express the early warning signs of the 2018 electoral tsunami. It is just that those on the Barisan Nasional side couldn't be bothered to listen, and many supporters on the Pakatan Harapan side probably thought it was outlandish to think that BN could be defeated against all the odds.

Kee Beng was one of the earliest to see the importance of the emergence of Dr Mahathir Mohamad as opposition leader and of his tactical moves to reconcile with Anwar Ibrahim.

Kee Beng's words are sharp and pointed: For instance, 'a resignation by Mahathir (from UMNO) is not a throwing in of the towel but a declaration of war.' But his concerns go beyond commenting on who would win and who would lose.

Nation building is what he cares about. How to shape a Malaysia that is at ease with itself and its multiethnic heritage in the rapidly changing world full of challenges – but also opportunities. Malaysia is not merely a collection of races and religions but a platform for individual citizens to thrive as citizens of a nation that they can all be proud of.

Kee Beng returned to the region in 2004 after having sojourned for more than two decades in Europe. I returned from Australia in 2005. Since our first meeting in Kuala Lumpur in 2005, we have in many ways participated in each other's careers, which somehow intertwined with the great changes in Malaysian politics that have been occurring since then. In the closing days of 2006, I was reading the then recently published *The Reluctant Politician* before it hit the bookshelves to become one of the most sold non-fiction books in Malaysian history, and through which Kee Beng became a favourite name among the Malaysian reading public. I remember clearly being at his house in Singapore in December 2007 telling him about my reluctance to contest in Penang as I wasn't sure about how much support could be gained in his hometown. I had no personal ties there.

So very much has happened ever since.

It is my great pleasure to have known Kee Beng all these years and to have him as one of my intellectual mentors.

In the 'New Malaysia', post-GE14, leaders will have to listen to the voices of public intellectuals such as Kee Beng, not only to broaden their horizons but also in order to see more clearly what they otherwise are too busy or too biased to see, before it is too late.

Introduction

Malaysia's Future is Redeemed

I co-authored a decade ago a book called *March 8: Eclipsing May 13*. What I was trying to do when I chose that title back in 2008 was to draw public attention to the centrality of history in understanding the confounding and exciting events that make up Malaysian politics. The twelfth general election that took place on 8 March 2008 was indeed a milestone that Malaysians will find hard to forget. However, that day simply signalled a shifting to a higher gear in a process that began many years ago, stretching back to 13 May 1969 and beyond. Its significance goes beyond its proximate spatial and tidal context.

That process continued after 2008 in fits and starts and finally came to fulfilment in the fourteenth general election that was held on 9 May 2018. That day, the Barisan Nasional government was toppled as the electorate chose with a resounding majority to end its six-decade-long period in power. As in all cases when a change in government had been waiting for too long, the change left many speechless and astounded. Much of how they had strategised their lives and how they thought in order to survive under that government became irrelevant overnight. Such is what a revolution feels like, even peaceful ones like the one that happened in Malaysia that day.

A spontaneous process of public re-education can now be expected to begin, and it will include much soul-searching and much throwing away of old ideas, old hates, old loves and old orientations.

To realise the full significance of what has come to pass, Malaysians will need to hit their history books. Sadly, not many history books about Malaysia exist which manage to capture at sufficient depth the many underlying dynamics contesting to direct the strange events that the country's political history is infamous for. Some active and analytical reading and researching is required now by each Malaysian interested in his or her own role in the present process of rebuilding the country.

Success for democracy in Malaysia is practically a prerequisite if countries in the region are to have any faith at all in a system where the people are free to choose and change their government. Born over six decades ago and equipped with much of the requirements for a functioning democracy, Malaya/Malaysia nevertheless quickly fell into the trap of identity politics and into a mindset of making do, getting by, biting the bullet, swallowing personal dignity and not hoping for too much. In the long run, such a path allowed for the abuse of power to grow. Luckily it was not allowed to grow forever and resistance to it became real enough to end it.

Accepting Diversity as an Asset

The multiculturalism that had always been the basis for Malaysia's economic and cultural strength was officially branded after 1969 as an intrinsic problem standing in the way of national harmony. Diversity was a curse, it was decided, and high psychological and conceptual walls began to be raised between the major ethnic groups. Political power became the prerogative of the majority group, or so it seemed. The truth was, political power stayed with the party that insisted by means fair and foul that it was the only proper representative of the Malays. For all Malaysians, other groups were to be considered an aberration they had to live with, not an asset to employ or enjoy.

A revision of sorts to the ideology of Malay-centric nationalism came with the introduction of Vision 2020 and Bangsa Malaysia by then-Prime Minister Mahathir Mohamad in the early 1990s. Fuelled by the prospect of unlimited economic growth, Malaysians were able to imagine that a gradual assimilation in identity and in culture was possible and should be preferred. The Asian Financial Crisis of 1997–98 put a stop to that.

I returned to the region in 2004, about six months after Tun Dr Mahathir Mohamad retired, and Abdullah Badawi had just been given a record-strong mandate in the 2004 general election to reform the country. Based then at the Institute of Southeast Asian Studies (ISEAS, now ISEAS – Yusof Ishak Institute), I was lucky enough to be able to study what everyone considered 'The Post-Mahathir Period' just when it was starting. Apart from publishing several books on the transitional 2008–18 period, I managed to put together five compilations of my own analyses of Malaysia's new era as it unfolded. These were *Era of Transition: Malaysia after Mahathir* (ISEAS, 2006); *Lost in Transition: Malaysia under Abdullah* (ISEAS & SIRD, 2008); *Arrested Reform: The Undoing of Abdullah Badawi* (REFSA, 2009); *Between UMNO and a Hard Place: The Najib Razak Era Begins* (ISEAS & REFSA, 2010); and *Done Making Do: 1Party Rule Ends in Malaysia* (ISEAS & Genta Media, 2013).

What we scholars and political analysts did not realise then was that we were in fact as much in a 'Pre-Mahathir Period' as we were in a 'Post-Mahathir Period'. My dear friend Barry Wain, who wrote the wonderfully researched biography on Mahathir, titled *Malaysian Maverick: Mahathir Mohamad in Turbulent Times* (Palgrave, 2009), never realised when he passed away several years ago that he would be needed to write part two on this incredibly resilient leader, who now returns to lead Malaysia at the age of 92. Quaintly, when Mahathir retired at the age of 78 in 2003, he was already the oldest prime minister Malaysia had ever had.

Not a Time for Cynics

This present compilation is therefore my seventh, and in a personally very satisfactory way, it rounds off the whole period between the first Mahathir period and the second Mahathir period. The transition away from UMNO's draconian rule that was constructed by Mahathir and abused by Najib finally happened. The system was so well developed against dismantlement that only with Mahathir at the helm of the opposition could the change actually be realised.

But it has now happened. And a new Mahathir era however short it may be, due to his advanced age, has begun.

We are all doomed to freedom, the French philosopher Jean-Paul Sartre famously said in clarification of his brand of existentialism. He suggests that freedom being a scary state to be in, we live our lives as if we are fettered even though we are not.

Whatever the case may be with Sartre's rather extreme claim, sensing freedom after a long period of cautious living under a regime that is racist in character and divisive in purpose heightens anxiety and uncertainty. The danger now lies in Malaysians treasuring their old habits, in their wish to keep old ways of relating to other Malaysians alive; or in them demanding that others change faster than they themselves are willing to change.

But then, nobody said it would be easy to topple a corrupt government. That has now been done and once done it appears like something that was inevitable. Developing new thoughts, strategies and habits to suit the free future that we wish for our children will not be a walk in the park.

A government falling is an event, however dramatic it may be, but building a country and a society that one can be proud of is a process and the work starts immediately in the individual's mind and heart. For example, cynicism has become a definite attitude among many Malaysians. Understandable though this may be, given how much disappointment several generations of Malaysians have had to endure, the future is not for cynics to build. It is built by people who dare to dream and hope, who are bold enough to forgive if not forget.

This collection of articles stretches back five years and I have chosen to include those that I feel have extra relevance now that a new age has begun for Malaysia. The story stretches over the second term of Najib Razak's administration from 2013 to 2018, but what these articles hope to highlight in response to the times are issues of nation-building and human morality relevant to the Malaysian situation today and in the future.

Before

PAKATAN HARAPAN

After All These Years, Malaysia Still Held Hostage[*]

In thinking about 2013, the year the Federation of Malaysia celebrates its fiftieth anniversary, one cannot but compare the national atmosphere to that in 2007, the year the Federation of Malaya celebrated its fiftieth anniversary.

I remember that the *New Straits Times* under Datuk Seri Kalimullah Hassan ran a week-long serialisation in January that year of my book *The Reluctant Politician: Tun Dr Ismail and His Time* (ISEAS, 2006) with the express purpose of putting the country into a contemplative mood and reminding Malaysians of what nation building is all about.

Given the faltering reform programme of then-Prime Minister Tun Abdullah Badawi, the year 2007 could not help but be a contemplative, and agitative, year for many Malaysians in any case. Be that as it may, to be fair to Abdullah, much change had come to the country after he took over from Tun Dr Mahathir Mohamad in October 2003.

Otherwise, the latter would not have been using his considerable political acumen back then to undermine his successor's position. Only Dr Mahathir's bad health that year limited his attacks on the prime minister.

Also noteworthy was how tame the UMNO general assembly was in 2007. Racial provocation was kept to a minimum amidst

---

[*] *The Malaysian Insider*, 4 September 2013.

7

rumours that elections would soon be called. However, Malaysia's first astronaut, Sheikh Mustaphar Sheikh Abdul Shukor, presented the Jalur Gemilang that he had taken into space to Abdullah at the UMNO meeting, signifying that whatever success the trip into space had been, it was an UMNO achievement, not a national triumph.

Inter-religious tension was also building up with the destruction of Hindu temples and the controversial burials of supposed Muslim converts.

The mood in 2007 was therefore generally more confused than contemplative and it soon led to open political activism in Kuala Lumpur.

The first Bersih demonstration took place on 10 November to highlight the need for electoral reforms, which was followed two weeks later by the Hindraf rally to demand rights for Hindus.

Already on 26 September that year, about 2,000 lawyers and their supporters calling for proper investigations into allegations of inappropriate appointments of judges had marched to the residence of the prime minister.

Six eventful years, another two Bersih demonstrations and two exciting elections later, much has changed.

The country now has a two-party system where the opposition has actually won the popular vote although without being able to take power; it now controls three states with a huge majority and has majority support in all urban centres.

The national atmosphere, however, remains as confused as ever. Dr Mahathir's son is now Mentri Besar of Kedah and is expected to aim for a top position within the party; inter-religious tensions persist between ever more hardened positions; race-baiting continues and the coming UMNO party elections are not expected to be anything close to being as tame as the 2007 party assembly; East Malaysian support now keeps the federal government in power; Chinese and urban support is solidly behind the opposition; the country is apparently no longer an oil exporter; violent crime has become shockingly common; and worries about the economy grow by the day, etc.

Datuk Seri Najib Razak has now received his own mandate to rule, no doubt, but it is an unconvincing one since he did lose the popular vote in West Malaysia and nationwide.

Whether the Prime Minister will survive the term, or even the year, is silently debated.

For now, his worst enemies are not in the opposition, but come from within his party. After all, nice-guy Abdullah was ousted 13 months after he won a weak electoral victory in 2008.

The year 2013 is also the tenth anniversary of Dr Mahathir's retirement as prime minister. Yet, Najib's administration, the second post-Mahathir government, continues to struggle with Dr Mahathir's dubious legacy and personal intrigues.

The political balance is certainly not stable. It may even be desperate, which is why there is so much talk about the need for a unity government that can straddle the incapacitating divides.

The political split down the middle has not been good for business confidence or public confidence in general. Sadly, it has not as yet thrown up effective leadership that can focus on national development instead of individual political careers and does not use disunity as its raison d'etre.

Therefore, for all concerned, there is a lot to contemplate this coming Malaysia Day and a lot of action required from political and business leaders to limit the opportunistic exaggeration of natural differences among Malaysians.

Without that, the country, and its economy, cannot begin to end its undeserved fate of being held hostage by politics that appeals to the basest instincts of its population.

Beyond the Nationalism Trap*

One thing that shocked me when I first went to Sweden for my studies 35 years ago was how dirty a word 'Nationalism' was in Western Europe. This reaction, I realised, was very much a reflection of how the concept was positively implanted in my mind while a schoolboy in Malaysia but it also demonstrated how greatly human experiences can differ in different parts of the world.

More importantly, it revealed to me how strongly we are intellectually captured by the language use of our times and our location.

But the Swedes are very proud of their country, so how come nationalism is frowned upon so badly? The same thing applied throughout Europe, at least until recently. Excessive immigration over the last two decades, coupled with declining economic fortunes and waning self-confidence has buoyed the ascendance of ultra-rightist groups in all countries throughout the continent.

So why was Nationalism so despised? Europe is after all the home continent of the nation state.

For starters, Europe was always a place of endless wars often fought ostensibly for religious reasons between feudal powers. The arrival of the nation state ideology helped to lower the frequencies of these tragedies but only to replace it soon after with non-religious types of rationale for conflict. The American Revolution and French Republicanism added the new phenomenon of 'government by the people'. The French case also brought into the equation the Left-Right

---

* *The Edge*, Malaysia, 28 October 2013.

Dimension that would define politics and political thinking for the next two centuries.

This conceptual division between Popular Mandate and Elite Rule expressed the rights of common people on the one hand and the role of the state on the other sharply. Once this gap was articulated, conflating the two poles anew became a necessary task.

The three major articulations in Europe of this mammoth mission to bridge the divide and achieve a functional modern system were Liberal Democracy, Communism and Fascism. While the Anglo-Saxon world championed the first, Stalin's Soviet Union perfected the second and Adolf Hitler developed the third to its insane conclusion. In Europe, it was basically these three actors who fought the Second World War.

In Asia, Japan's brand of state fascism ran riot throughout the region, rhetorically championing nationalism in the lands it took from the European colonialists.

While the National Socialism of the Third Reich died with Hitler, Fascism lived on in Franco's Spain until 1975 and Nationalist Communism of Stalin continued in Eastern Europe until the early 1990s.

Nationalism in the rest of Europe after 1945 came to be understood with disdain as the longing of the Nation State for purity and autonomy taken to pathological lengths. It is after all always a defensive posture, as is evidenced today in its return in the form of right-wing anti-immigrant groups.

In Malaysia, nationalism was, and for many still is, the most highly rated attitude for a citizen to adopt.

There are obvious reasons for this, given the historical and socio-political context in which Malaysia came into being. Constructing a new country out of nine sultanates, the three parts of the Straits Settlements, with Sabah and Sarawak on top of that, was a more daunting task than we can imagine today. Furthermore, the contest was also against other powerful '-isms', especially Communism and Pan-Indonesianism. These threatened to posit what are Malaysia's states today in a larger framework and would have diminished these territories' importance and uniqueness.

Putting a new regime in place of the retreating British required a rallying idea; and what better than the very fashionable image of a new nation to whom all should swear allegiance. Malayan nationalism was thus born.

It is no coincidence that the path to independence became much easier after Malaysia's major political party, UMNO, decided under Tengku Abdul Rahman to change its slogan from the provincial 'Hidup Melayu' [Long Live the Malays] to the inclusive 'Merdeka' [Independence].

But already in that transition, one can see the problem that Malaysia still lives with today. Is Malaysia the political expression of the prescriptive majority called 'Melayu' [later stretched to become 'Bumiputera'], or is it the arena in which the multi-ethnic nation of 'Malaysians' is to evolve?

Nationalism in essence, and most evidently so in its narrow ethnocentric sense, is defensive and fearful, and understood simplistically and applied arrogantly very quickly shows strong fascist tendencies. The issue is therefore a philosophical one.

What Malaysia needs today is to accept the regional and global context that sustains it and work out as best it can a suitable balance between Popular Mandate and Elite Rule which is clearly less belaboured and less painful than the cul-de-sac alleyway it has backed itself into.

Federating Malaysia — A Continuous and Troubled Process*

PM's cover story this month is about East Malaysia and how unknown a territory it has always been to Malaysians on the peninsula. To start with, we need to remind ourselves of how troubled the beginnings of the Federation of Malaya actually were – and I don't only mean the Indonesian decision to initiate undeclared war against the new polity.

The situation in the region in the two decades following the end of the Japanese Occupation of Southeast Asia, was fragile whichever way you look at it: states were emerging without clear ideas about what nations they would represent or craft or about what territorial borders for that matter; and international communism was seriously challenging the world order in the wake of the failure by Germany, Italy and Japan to do the same.

Furthermore, the old colonial powers were in hasty retreat from the region and were therefore fully focused on political and military rear-guard actions. America had just inherited the front position where the western world was concerned.

That is the larger picture.

The influence that global conflicts and late-colonial expediencies had on Malaysia's constitution and history was undeniably great. However, local political, legal and notional factors impacting the nature of the new federation turn out to have left more traumatic

---

* Editorial, *Penang Monthly*, April 2014.

aftereffects than regional events like the Konfrontasi or the Vietnam War have done.

Despite the close proximity and the common history, Singapore fitted quite uncomfortably into Malaya at that point. Its unionist movement and labour laws were much more developed than on the peninsular mainland; the largely Chinese population on the island outnumbered all over communities taken together by 875,000; and the two education systems were politically incompatible.

As we know, the split between the Federation of Malaysia and Singapore came in 1965 after two years of mutual enmity and with fear of civil war in the air. Sabah and Sarawak stayed within the Federation till today.

Unlike Singapore, the states in Borneo were underpopulated and undeveloped territories and politically underdeveloped in 1963; and when they co-founded the Federation were granted a huge overrepresentation in parliamentary seats. Singapore's 1,750,000 persons gave it 15 members of parliament while Sabah and Sarawak together, with a population of about 850,000 would have 40. Malaya would have 104 representatives.

A racial game of numbers was obviously being played as well, stamping ethnicity deeper into the federation's DNA.

By most accounts, the East Malaysian states were 'not ready for independence', and given the global political climate then, the powerful stakeholders thought it best to stake a claim an early over the huge expanse of land. As Tengku Abdul Rahman Putra, Malaysia's first Prime Minister, noted: 'Time is not on our side. The important aspect of the Malaysian ideal, as I see it, is that it will enable the Borneo territories to transform their present colonial status to self-government for themselves and absolute independence in Malaya simultaneously, and baulk the Communist attempt to capture these territories.'

There was to his mind, a grave need to absorb Sabah and Sarawak in order to nurture them towards political maturity.

The case of Brunei is another convoluted story where an armed revolt was staged by A.M. Azahari, who wished for the uniting of Sabah, Brunei and Sarawak under one Sultan.

These are all just part of an exciting story about colonial withdrawal from a region where nation-states were a conceptual import.

In the search for self-understanding and inspiration for enlightened policies, Malaysians–East and West– would do well to learn more about their own history.

Funeral for a True Son of Penang*

The morning was soft and cloudy, but only for a while. By 10:00 am, the sun was blazing and having its usual relentless way with Penangites. Perhaps as many as 20,000 of us were already gathered outside the Dewan Sri Pinang, where the body of one of Penang's most beloved sons had been lying in state since 8:00 am that Sunday, 20 April 2014.

Karpal Singh, respected lawyer, fiery Member of Parliament for Bukit Gelugor and foe of countless bigots is no more. He was killed in a traffic accident on the North-South Highway in the first hour of 17 April.

Huge throngs of people who three days later lined the streets around the State Assembly Hall, the courts and St Xavier's Institute to wave goodbye and to shout 'Karpal Singh' one last time, following thousands of others who had over the two nights before the funeral visited his family home in Western Road to pay their respects. Many made the trip from as far away as Johor to join fellow countrymen and countrywomen to publicly mourn Karpal Singh and who felt that this was the least they could do for a man whose fighting spirit had always been inspirational.

We should certainly pause and ponder why so many Malaysians and Penangites felt such a strong need to come together. I am sure there is a whole range of reasons, but chief among these has to be the iconic status achieved by the man. He had simply come to symbolise the stand against bigotry and abuse of the law which the country has been suffering from for so long.

---

* Editorial, *Penang Monthly*, May 2014.

His belief that respect for the law is the necessary foundation for a just society and for protection of human rights was something that has had immediate appeal to people of all classes. His bravery in speaking back to arrogant power and the directness of his words carried immediate appeal in a society given to hushed compromise and feudal diffidence.

These values held so strongly in him certainly resonated well in Penang, whose people struggled to consider it liberal and modern. In all ways, Karpal Singh was indeed a true son of Penang – he represented Penang values with great ease. In fact, he amplified them more loudly than anyone else.

In that way, perhaps his persona as an activist lawyer was what endeared him to common folk more than his role as a bold politician. But once that is said, it does seem trivial to even try to separate the different parts of the man. He was in the thick of so many battles over the decades and he was in the consciousness of Malaysians for such a long time that he was in truth simply 'Karpal Singh', the one and only, irreplaceable and unique.

He will be sorely missed. Looking back, we find solace in the fact that his sturdy example inspired so many young people that we know for sure that Malaysia would have been a worse place without him.

The Tiger of Jelutong may roar no more, but I certainly hear the roll of that thunder amplified in countless hearts. Whether that echo will grow in volume depends on new champions of the values he represented so excellently.

Let's Work Out What Malaysia Is Good For*

A wave of pessimism and dejection has been pervading Malaysia for quite a long time now. Exactly when it started is hard to say, but what has been obvious is that whatever potential lines of division that can be found in the diversity that characterises the country have recently been made more salient.

Relatedly, the types of criminality seem to have become harsher, suggesting that the social fabric is being worn very thin and that the economic situation for the lower classes has worsened dramatically. The recent abduction and beheading of a two-year-old girl in Kuala Lumpur stunned the country.

Homelessness has increased with as many as 1,500 people not only roaming the streets of Kuala Lumpur with no shelter but also being accused of preferring stealing and begging to 'a normal life'. The latter bizarre verdict reportedly came from no one less important than the country's Minister for Women, Family and Community Development.

The planned implementation of a federal goods and services tax regime in April next year to ease state budgetary imbalances, whether well-advised or not, is not expected to help the less fortunate either.

Apart from deteriorating socio-economic conditions, inter-ethnic and inter-faith relations have been widening, pushed by small extremist groups with ties to the dominant party claiming mass media coverage

---

* *The Edge*, Malaysia, 30 July 2014.

for themselves way beyond their due – and certainly way beyond the merit of their arguments.

Religious authorities have also been overly eager in policing improprieties in Malaysia's highly pluralistic society, in one case taking Malaysians back to the trauma of observing a non-Muslim funeral being disrupted by Muslim authorities that took the deceased away from her family with the claim that she was a converted Muslim. The Penang State Shariah court rejected this claim a couple of days later. Such cases of 'body snatching' at funerals grabbed the headlines frequently several years ago causing great damage to inter-faith trust.

The ban on the use of certain words considered the monopoly of Muslims has also upset non-Muslims greatly, again undermining trust between the diverse communities that constitute the population of the Malaysian federation.

All in all, the present atmosphere in Malaysia is not conducive at all to any celebration of its ethnic diversity or its substantial economic potential. Many are blaming the quality of leadership of its present government, which tends to prefer silence to pronouncements of clear principles, especially in dealing with religious and ethnic issues. No doubt, the confused handling by the government of the disappearance of Malaysia Airlines' MH370 in May, and the international criticism it received, weakened its self-confidence further.

Reticence as policy on the part of the government comes at a time when the ruling coalition faces a newly emerged civil society eagerly backed by influential blogs and web newspapers and a young and articulate opposition that does not look like going away anytime soon.

For the moment, the country seems unable to look beyond itself despite the huge challenges facing its economy and the deterioration of its once shiny image in the world. Instead it struggles over issues such as which word should or should not be used by whom, which family should or should not bury which of its members, and can one be seditious when claiming to be championing Malay rights or Muslim values.

Simply put, Malaysia has not been able to get out of the social and political melancholy precipitated by the economic depression it suffered in 1998. The defence mechanism of its establishment has been too strong and its conservatism too immediate.

Although significant political and social changes have taken place since then, the elite of the country has not managed to conjure a new self-image and a vision for the country that is more expressive of the new situation. Instead, it has allowed public discourses to descend into incoherence and bigotry.

Some sense of loss is understandable in times of change, but somewhere, the paralysis has to stop. This failure to rise above the fray, to see beyond daily squabbles is Malaysia's biggest challenge today.

Now, Malaysia is to hold the ASEAN chairmanship next year. This means it is the last runner in the relay race towards Southeast Asia's regional economic integration. It will oversee the tying of loose ends in this enormously important process. Furthermore, it will most probably be elected a non-permanent member of the United Nations' Security Council in 2015. Its candidacy was forwarded by ASEAN, and at the moment, no other Asia Pacific country is in the running. Chances are good that Malaysia will get into the Council, its first time since 2000.

While it is often said, on good grounds, that one's home should be in order before one can speak with authority outside it, the dynamics can also go the other way. There is potential for the Malaysian government in the coming two years at least to not only rebuild its international image but also to allow that exercise to affect the country's self-image and stimulate a broad public consensus on what Malaysia is about. Tired slogans like One Malaysia or sad to say, even Vision 2020, will no longer work. They are overused and the attempts to give them substance have been too frail.

The question for Wisma Putra to ask itself, the question for the government to raise even among its supporters and the question citizens should investigate is, What's Malaysia Good For? Allowing public discourses to degrade as unceremoniously as it has been doing over the last few years and allowing social cohesion to unravel for want of national goals is a dangerous and destructive path for the government to take.

Once Malaysia can work out what it is good for in the world – and this can best be done based on the common sense that common Malaysians once took for granted – can it stand proud again as the unique creation that it is.

7

The Unity Fetish*

fe•tish
noun \ 'fe-tish also 'fē-
: a strong and unusual need or desire for something
: a need or desire for an object, body part or activity for sexual excitement
: an object that is believed to have magical powers

The Collective Individual

Malaysia is a land of diversity. However, the need to adopt the nation-state structure to replace colonialism disposed the country's post-colonial leaders to see its diversity as a weakness – in fact, as potential dynamite.

No doubt, much of that diversity was politically salient and basically of a divisive nature. Agendas and values among potential nation builders did differ greatly and the two forces that had, on good grounds, always been thought to be most dangerous were communalism and communism.

The latter is now passé, while the former has been heavily enhanced, and has left the country with a political structure pathologically fixated with ethnicity – a condition that in recent years has become aggravated by religion.

Over the last half-century, with so much of the country's governing logic being based on ethnic affiliations, it has not been easy for

---

* Cover story, *Penang Monthly*, February 2015.

Malaysians to appreciate diversities in general as something that can be positive. In fact, it is no exaggeration to say that most differences today, including in viewpoints, are seen through a racial lens. Should a Malay not agree with the principle of Malay supremacy, he or she is loudly suspected of being a race traitor. And if his understanding of Islamic behaviour differs from the state-sanctioned one, then he is in the eyes of the authorities on the way to being an apostate, or to jail.

This goes for the other races as well, except that if truth be told, it is the Malay community that has been exposed most strongly to collective identity manipulation. In the Constitution, it is already stated what characterises a Malay. This extraordinary attempt to define ethnicity legally definition may have seemed a good political strategy, but it does involve over time a minimising of individual space for the sake of the political advantage of the community as understood, and as led and represented, by a select group of leaders.

But with the irrefutable rise of a political opposition that won 51 per cent of the popular vote in 2013, aided no doubt by vast advancements in ICT and by the urbanising of daily life for a majority of citizens, a sense of individual empowerment has spread to challenge the collective ethnic and religious identity that had regimented Malaysian politics for so long.

This fact is easily missed if one thinks of politics only in party and coalition terms. But if seen in the fluid terms needed to describe contemporary social and physical mobility, the liberation of information flow and the diversity of individual fates, Malaysian society has changed in radical ways.

At the same time, such change has first to deal with the complexities of the past, mainly the bad press that diversity has been getting. In short, diversity was ethnicised, collectivised and, therefore, problematised to such an extent that individual fates and uniqueness of individual lives were dismissed from political agendas. What this means is that Malaysians were drilled to think of themselves as members of an ethnic group first, before they are individuals with unique experiences.

This may have been the common destiny of societies suddenly grouped or turned into new political entities, of which there were many in Asia and Africa following the Second World War. But what this also did was to make them think that such was the inescapable lot of Third World peoples.

That is the socio-psychological legacy of post-colonial nationalism as found in these parts of the world. But now, with the majority of the population in these countries being born long after independence, a point is being reached where the strategies of old misrepresent the desires of the present. This is a global phenomenon, but let me keep to Malaysia here.

Allow me to recognise the present moment in Malaysian history as the tail end of the nationalist era. That is just another way of describing what many have called a crossroads; a crossroads at which the country has found itself since the turn of the century.

In the early period of Malaysian nation building, the major concerns were about the viability of the new entity, meaning the defining of the new polity and whether or not it could be consolidated. It was about the hasty grouping together into one country of what in effect were disparate societies, disparate polities and disparate economies.

Overnight, out of what were disparate consciousnesses or mindsets, we set about creating a national citizenry (complete with national army, national police, national education), a national government, national borders which were to be jealously guarded and – this is most overlooked – a national economy out of very disparate economies. We also immediately made some national enemies and we entered into security alliances and a host of other international arrangements to secure recognition and safety.

That was the nationalist era. We joined the global family of nation-states. We learned to think in unifying and regimenting terms for fear that a lack of uniformity would spell disaster.

Nation or State?

Now, 'nation-state' is the important word here. We began building a nation and building a state both at the same time. The two processes are different things, and identifying the key practices for national economic development was the overarching concern. (By 'state', I mean the apparatus of the state, be this central or provincial, and not as in 'Kedah', 'Kelantan' or 'Johor').

Let me say a few words on what the divides in Malaysia are and let us remind ourselves that divides are not naturally politically salient.

Structurally, race and religion seem the most important divides in Malaysia. This is deeply expressed in the political party structure, and even in the Constitution, not to mention the sultanate-based state polity in nine of the 13 states. And over the years, this has deeply influenced the education system, the civil service and the choice of foreign influences.

Then there is the development divide, the income divide and the modernity divide (by the latter I mean functionality in the global capitalist, scientific and technological world), not to mention cultural divides, based partly on ethnicity, partly on class, partly on urbanity, partly on education and a host of other parameters.

Nation building is about generating identity, but if this process does not seek to be inclusive of all Malaysians, then one is basically generating deep emotional divisions with the populace. This can of course be a path consciously chosen by nation builders, with disunity being considered by them as a necessary price to pay for the time being.

State building on the other hand is the creation of rules, regulations and legislations, and administrative structures that apply to all. In that way, this process is inclusive. Knowing rules that apply equally to everyone becomes the unifying factor. Nothing emotional about it.

Let us take the issue of education to illustrate the difference. Education in the nation-building process will be strongly concerned with the language of instruction, about values learning, about national history. It will be about defining the past, present and future of ethnic identification and division. Education in the state-building process, in turn, will be about providing opportunities for all, about functional knowledge, about creating citizens to fill roles within the economy and the civil service.

One without the other leads to undesirable effects: too much nation building exaggerates group attachment and too much state building does the opposite.

The question to ask of Malaysians at this time is, 'How should state building and nation building be rebalanced to remedy earlier ills?'

Malaysia is not alone in this complicated process, and although there are tight limits to how much one can compare countries or state and nation-building processes, there is much that can be learned from the experiences of other countries:

1. If your society is divided by religion, you need a secular state to unite you;

2. If your society is disjointed by race, you need a legalist state to referee you, and;

3. If your society is separated by class, you need a redistributive state to consolidate you.

State building is a largely technical matter, while nation building is a psychological one. A successful balance between the two, we have to assume, can achieve economic growth that is potentially inclusive (meaning social mobility), provide national security and keep serious internal conflicts at bay.

Nation building is about identity; while state building is about predictability, order and functionality. The first requires prolonged emotional manipulation, the other cumulative technical knowledge. In Malaysia, since 1970 at least, the trend had moved from state building to nation building and the country has had to suffer the latter's strong tendency – in fact inherent need – to generate tension and conflict.

I would argue that the discursive changes needed for Malaysia to enter a post-nationalist period include:

1. Seeing Malaysia's development process within regional and global contexts whose forces it cannot escape but from which it can instead draw much benefit; and

2. Accepting a notion of sufficient, and not total, commonality and uniformity.

Having race-based parties running the state has over time, especially given the constraints on debate that the post-1971 parliament placed on society, led to the effective capture of the state by the dominant race-based party. Malaysia's nation building and state building became the prerogative, and even the monopoly, of UMNO and its allies. This has conserved and nursed the fear of social disunity and national disaster, which was understandable in the early years, and turned it into a fetish. Operationally, this has seen the transforming of the socioeconomic and pragmatic notion of Malay special position into the ideological and essentialist notion of Malay special rights.

Much of the political opposition in Malaysia today is about a widespread endeavour to escape from the debilitating party power structure and this discursive stranglehold. This includes a wide variety of NGOs as well, which is a good reminder of how, while the country over the years has been highlighting some chosen divisions and ignoring others, new ones have appeared, inspired by changes in the world in general. This includes environmental concerns, refugee situations and illegal workers.

Treating Fetishism

The Unity Fetish – the assumption that more unity is better than less – is best cured through the search for Sufficient Communality, the point where diversity is beneficial and more unity brings discord. The Unity Fetish, like all fetishes, cannot be satisfied. There is no point at which success can be declared to have been achieved. And so, discord is its real goal.

Building a country is like building a house. Given the diversities and divisions that exist among those who are to populate this house, one has to decide on the right size of house, the right combination of rooms and the right facilities to provide. The point is to get the right architecture – the right fengshui – for the house to flourish and be at peace.

Building too small a house will simply generate tensions and conflicts that may tear it apart.

Again, we should not get too fixated on bringing people together, but with giving them space. One can have one's cake and eat it too if one can find the right distance at which disparate groups can relate to each other. Over time, and given the necessary facilities for interaction, etc., social integration has a good chance of happening. The issue is time. Society needs time to hybridise, meaning that identity is really organic in essence and cannot be defined in advance. This also reminds us that clear, and therefore false definitions of identity, be they embedded in the Constitution, in legal practice or in bureaucratic regulations, act against hybridisation.

The long-term effects of such collectivisation of public identity cannot be conducive to creativity and to the sense of individual empowerment that undergirds creativity and personal confidence.

Daily life in a pluralistic society naturally leads to interactions that leave everyone mutually affected. This is the best possible process through which not only shared understanding can be achieved but also a strong realisation that individual identity is tentative in nature and is forever shifting.

Collective identities are a demand from without, while individual identity is a personally lived experience.

In conclusion, excessive concern with 'unity' is problematic for various reasons. It aims to create an unchanging social and political structure within which 'unity' is minimally threatened. Such a goal, being assimilative in effect, tends to increase and perpetuate tension between communities. Also, it contains the ambition for cultural and thought uniformity. The fluid nature of social cohesion is denied, and last but not least, squeezing society into as few dimensions as possible and pulling it as much as possible away from the multidimensional reality that we actually live in.

The unity fetish tends to disunite by playing an 'including by excluding' game and yet at the same time whomever it includes is not necessarily privileged because the including process amounts in the long run to a coercive and tightening definition of the included individual.

8

When the National Narrative Loses the Script*

Malaysia is in serious trouble today because the different narratives that have been driving politics in the country for more than half a century have come into direct conflict with each other. This shows more clearly than ever that what was always important for social peace in the country was a balance between contradictory narratives.

While a narrative is simply an account that connects chosen events and experiences in a story-like fashion, one that seeks to describe a nation is something quite different because it subscribes roles and identities to individuals and groups. It is also one that has to stimulate pride and participation in its citizens and provides a clear sense of historical place for the nation as a whole.

Essentially, a good national story is one that is inclusive of as many of the inhabitants as possible since the country requires sufficient harmony for the economy to function.

But there are abundant cases where minorities are kept outside the mainstream, or a given secondary or peripheral identities. As extreme examples, we have the apartheid regime in South Africa which suppressed the numerical majority (but economic minority) and the Nazis in Hitler's Germany of course, which had 'final solutions' for 'inferior and harmful minorities' at the lower end of its ethnic hierarchy.

---

* *The Edge*, Malaysia, April 2015.

It is true that the national storyline is seldom dictated by a single powerful regime. Instead, what we have are endless negotiations and contestations between different national scripts. In modern times, with citizens enjoying broad exposure to the world, high educational levels and free information flows, this seems quite inescapable.

That is why democracy in some form seems such a necessary thing. It allows for different scripts to vie with each other by non-violent means. Otherwise, the contentions tend to take an all-or-nothing form. That way lies chaos, civil war and economic stagnation.

Where Malaysia is concerned, what does the history of this balancing of narratives look like?

On 16 September 1963, the Federation of Malaysia was born through agreements between the Federation of Malaya, the recently self-ruling British crown colony of Singapore and the British territories of Sabah and Sarawak. And on 9 August 1965, Singapore separated from the federation.

Working backwards then, we see how the complex political situation on the peninsula harmonised in the 1950s to a good enough extent for independence to be peacefully achieved. This was done through the consociational solution we know as the Alliance. In winning electoral support, in being fully anti-communist and most importantly, in being able to present a working multi-ethnic model of cooperation to the British, the Alliance could not be denied the right to rule an independent Malaya.

The solution was ingenious. Here are the main ethnic groups represented each by a party championing its interest and these collaborate with each other in ruling the country. Nice and neat, and it left the communists with no effective counter-move.

But all this happened without Singapore, which the British had kept as a crown colony even as it retreated from its Malayan Union idea to accept the Federation of Malaya as its replacement in 1948. Something had to be done about Singapore and the solution in 1963 was to create Malaysia, together with Sabah and Sarawak.

In those two years that Singapore was in Malaysia, we saw how conflicting narratives could not find a peaceful way of living with each other. The solution left a country consisting not only of a population where the non-bumiputeras were numerically strong but also one that was ethnically much more complex than before 1963.

Emotions ran high as the Alliance model gained a huge drop in support in the 1969 elections and rioting broke out. By 1974, a new model had replaced it. But this was possible only after a lot of legislative restrictions and political arm-twisting was done. From then on, Malaysia enjoyed an uneasy peace where the balance between narratives was possible only because much less was now allowed expression.

But it worked and the population learned to live with the constraints. The country went on to enjoy some golden years of growth and influence during the early 1990s. The New Economic Policy that was developed in the early 1970s to further the Malays, development was tempered with Vision 2020 and the Bangsa Malaysia discourses after 1990; and it provided a good enough balance of narratives for the country to continue growing peacefully.

The Asian financial crisis of 1997–98 shook that balance and out of that grew the call for reforms in governance. This grew strong enough to convince Tun Dr Mahathir Mohamad to retire if his party was to stay in power and we saw how his successor, Abdullah Badawi, had the space to respond effectively to this new movement with his series of reforms.

The results of the 2004 elections showed that a new balance was in fact within reach. But Abdullah failed to see his reforms through due to resistance from within his own coalition, and the results of the 2008 elections showed that the moment had passed and a new balance would not be gained so easily.

Abdullah's successor, Najib Razak, continued in like vein with his transformation programmes and we saw how that failed dismally as well in 2013 in finding a new balance of narratives.

What has been happening since 2008 and what has been seen as the emergence of a two-party system, is Malaysia caught in what I call 'The Middle Outcome Trap', where the population is split right down the middle into two halves.

The country's lack of a new workable compromise, a lasting balance, between national narratives, is therefore a serious one. The longer this situation continues, the greater the risk that the digging in of positions will undermine the structure of the state itself.

With Islamisation fervour being allowed to take hold and alienating Muslims and non-Muslims from the political process, it is apparent that the central government lacks the confidence or will to seek a new balance and seems to see the situation as unchangeable, and so has decided simply to survive from scandal to scandal and crisis to crisis.

9

Let's Be Cosmopolitan and Leave Multi-ethnicity Behind*

It is fascinating how seemingly innocuous words actually are not. Especially those that sound neutral, even ethically positive. That is why the sage never thinks in haste, because he knows the words that bear his thoughts cannot be trusted and his listener's ability to understand him the way he wishes to be understood must always be doubted.

Take 'multi-ethnic' for example. We often consider that term to be a practical synonym for 'pluralism' or 'multicultural'. And so, we move on from that concept to begin dreaming about celebrating diversity based on multi-ethnicity. And we are then exasperated by how impossible that seems to be.

I suspect the basic problem is that 'multi-ethnic' is actually a highly conservative term. Its major connotations are static and ignore the evolving nature of individual identities in favour of collectivising humans under simple groupings.

Revealingly, after the term 'race' became taboo in social scientific circles following the end of the Second World War, 'ethnicity' was recruited instead to replace it. In Malaysia, we now use those two as synonyms, as we do with 'multi-racial' and 'multi-ethnic'.

Putting together disparate units that are in the process starkly distinguished from each other does not bode well for the harmony of the whole. There is a contradiction herein that should warn us to have low expectations. The association between the groups is encouraged

---

* Editorial, *Penang Monthly*, April 2015.

to be cultural or religious and is about treating each other as members and representatives of distinct groups. This collective identity approach to social life is a defensive and conflict-oriented one that cannot but breed caution and fear rather than celebration and enjoyment. If you ask me, that is where racism has its roots.

The future is urban

There is also the aspect of existential space. If we assume rurality as the backdrop for modern social interactions, then we are assuming that there is sufficient space for problematic differences to exist at a safe distance from each other. On the other hand, if we assume urbanity instead as the present and definitely the future nature of Malaysian society, then we must deal with the fact that there is simply not enough existential space for static divisions to be able to co-exist harmoniously.

And so, thinking in terms of 'multi-ethnicity' and the like will not work. It is a remnant of our past. Just as the race-based nature of so many of the country's national parties is an embarrassing heritage.

Modernity is an urban phenomenon. I will not need to argue this point; the evidence in support of this is abundant, ranging from the increasing proportion of people living in cities and from the growth of mega-cities as economic centres. And since we must assume urbanity as our future state, we have to take on the challenge of social harmony in cramped spaces. Which means we had better stop thinking in haste and instead consider the effective connotations of the terms we pick to anchor national discourses and try to choose words that will foster attitudes conducive to harmony in urban life.

Let me suggest that the next time you feel like saying 'multi-ethnic' or 'multiracial', you use the word 'cosmopolitan' instead. We have a multi-ethnic society already. We describe it as such and we conserve it as such. What we want is something beyond that. 'Cosmopolitan' sounds just about right.

This term does not highlight collective identities and it does not force social interactions onto one or two politically favoured dimensions. It is open-ended and it is individual-friendly.

Most importantly, it is inclusive of non-collective identities the way 'multi-ethnic' is not.

10

Noses Don't Grow Back*

It is very sad that the state of Penang is being ignored in the 11th Malaysia Plan (2016–20). None of the infrastructure projects the Penang government presented for financial support has been accepted by the federal government. Putrajaya seems to imagine that Malaysia will reach advanced nation status by 2020 without Penang's contribution; instead KL, Johor Bahru, Kuching and Kota Kinabalu are declared the growth catalyst cities, and will therefore receive central support.

Penang Chief Minister Lim Guan Eng was right to be outraged, as all Penangites are.

They do not seem surprised by the fact that the federal government is willing to lower the country's chances of achieving advanced nation status just for the pleasure of punishing its stepchild state.

Cutting your nose to spite your face is not something sane people do.

Among the first things to happen following Malaysia's first general elections in 1964 was the suspension of local government elections. This affected Penang greatly. Local government in the state had been responsible 'in advancing progressive policies such as social housing and major public infrastructure projects such as drainage, public toilets (a novel idea at that time), mobile clinics and even a dam.' (See *Penang Monthly's* cover story for April 2015, p. 35).

---

* Editorial, *Penang Monthly*, June 2015.

This was followed by the steady withdrawal of the free port status that Penang had always enjoyed. This spiked further the unemployment that the state was already suffering in the late 1960s, exacerbated by the crisis that followed the huge devaluation of the British Pound on 18 November 1967. The Penang riots of 1968 were very much a result of severe economic dejection.

We forget today how bad things actually were for Penang back in the days and how many of the state's sons and daughters had to leave for what they could only hope were greener pastures either to the Klang Valley or beyond.

The depressed socioeconomic situation of the times sufficiently explains the Gerakan phenomenon – how this party, Partai Gerakan Rakyat, founded only on 24 March 1968 by a hotchpotch of failing politicians and idealist academics, could take power in Penang in May 1969, less than 14 months after it came into being.

Obviously, the time was right. The fruit was ripe and ready to fall.

Penang's people had to suffer high unemployment for another few years, however, further overwhelmed by the New Economic Policy initiated under the Second Malaysia Plan (1971–75). Things looked really gloomy then.

It was thanks to the resourcefulness of the new Chief Minister Tun Dr Lim Chong Eu that Penang's economy could turn around. He managed to create the free trade zone that ever since then has been the main driver of growth in the state, alongside tourism.

Dato' Seri Chet Singh, the general manager of the Penang Development Corporation formed then to industrialise and modernise the state, remembers how getting permission to establish a free trade zone was practically impossible. It was only through direct dialogue with Tun Abdul Razak Hussein, who was then running the country while Parliament remained suspended, that it could be achieved:

He came up for a visit and we took him out to the area designated for the free trade zone. He called his officer over and sternly told him to take note. He pointed with his cane a few times to mark out the area we had suggested and there on the spot, he declared the area a free trade zone. That was that. He cut through all the red tape and all the institutional resistance, literally in one fell swoop. On realising that success in Penang would bring greater success to the country, he fully supported us.

A wise man knows that there are good reasons why his nose is placed right in the middle of his face. And cutting it off is not something one should ever contemplate.

In any case, speaking of Vision 2020, what has been forgotten is that the national dream as presented by Tun Dr Mahathir Mohamad 25 years ago was more than simply a hope of economic advancement. It was about the attainment of a society, a Malaysia, that is at peace with itself and that is proud of its inevitable diversity.

11

Mahathir's Bersatu is Best Understood as an NGO*

The recent decision by the 91-year-old former Malaysian Prime Minister Mahathir Mohamad and his closest supporters to form a new political party understandably raised many eyebrows. This incomprehension turned into indignation when it was announced that the party, Parti Pribumi Bersatu Malaysia (Bersatu), will be a Malay-based one and non-Malays can only be associate members.

The pertinent question the founding of Bersatu appears to raise is whether racial affinity is really something one can ignore in politics be it in Malaysia or elsewhere. And if yes, to what extent. However, the issue is another.

The opposition parties had been growing stronger over the last decade but never strong enough, and with that, it has become clear that Barisan Nasional, the ruling coalition, remains in power because it has the rural vote. Even with the scandals surrounding 1MDB, Prime Minister Najib Razak's government appears unassailable still.

The claim that Malaysians are moving away from race politics is undeniably truer of urban areas than of the kampongs. Is the hold that UMNO has in the rural areas exercised through patronage politics alone, as multiracialists would like to believe, or is it more profoundly because UMNO is seen by many Malays as the champion of their race, no matter how bad its recent performance has been?

---

* ISEAS Commentary 2016/47, 19 August 2016.

Bersatu is essentially not in effect to be seen as an ordinary political party. It is best understood as a one-issue non-government organisation (NGO). And its goal is the toppling of Najib. In the context of its founding, it could not have been anything other than a race-based party and its simple strategy is to win votes away from UMNO and convince rural voters that there can be more than one Malay champion.

In that sense, Bersatu has a progressive role to play.

Before

9 MAY
2018

12

Racialising the Un-racialisable: What is the Red Shirt Rally All About?*

Following the Red-Shirt rally in Kuala Lumpur on 16 September, discussions have been rife that the government of Prime Minister Najib Razak was 'playing the racial card' to bolster support and to distract the public, especially its Malay supporters, from distressing issues at hand.

It is true that the demonstration was a purely Malay rally, but what is essential to note is that while the initial impulse to organise it came from people who were undoubtedly trying to highlight and deepen the racial divide, by the time the event did take place, much of that had been deftly turned into a show of support for the beleaguered prime minister by his staunchest followers.

In the end, few incidents took place and the riot police did not have much trouble keeping rowdy demonstrators at bay, who were symbolically trying to get into the city's Chinatown.

This is an important point to highlight. The racialising did not spread.

The demonstration was an angry reaction by Mr Najib supporters to the anti-Najib Bersih 4.0 rally that took place on 29–30 August. Notwithstanding the huge turnout at that two-day event, some mass

---

* *TODAY* newspaper, Singapore, 28 September 2015.

media outlets had focused on the proportionately low number of Malay participants at the Bersih rally.

This in sadly typical of Malaysian journalism, in fact—whatever happens, look for the racial aspect first.

What should be read out of this is that the Bersih Movement has been very successful in achieving its main long-term goal. This is not so much electoral reforms as the gradual shifting of the national discourse away from persistent racial issues over to a passion for democratic governance instead.

Ever since it was formed by a large group of civil society organisations and opposition parties, Bersih (short for Gabungan Pilihanraya Bersih dan Adil—the Coalition for Clean and Fair Elections) has relied for support on its non-racial agenda of electoral reforms.

The latest version of its reforms are (1) free and fair elections; (2) a clean government; (3) the right to dissent; (4) strengthening parliamentary democracy; and (5) saving the Malaysian economy. These are generally so technical and generic in nature that one would be hard put to turn them into racial issues.

This was in essence what the red shirts tried to do. They were not simply expressing Malay anger, not simply demanding respect for Malays and not simply standing up to perceived threats from non-Malays. And they were not simply showing support for Mr Najib. They were most essentially trying to racialise something quite un-racialisable.

After the first Bersih rally in 2007, the opposition parties, on gaining control of several state governments, decided not to be directly involved in the movement. This led to the forming of the organisation, Bersih 2.0, which has since organised three more rallies, in 2011, 2012 and most recently in August 2015.

In all of the first three rallies, race did not manifest itself because the support was across the board. All communities were supporting them and that explains the picnic atmosphere that has come to characterise these rallies. What made Bersih 4.0 different was that it came at a time when Parti Islam Se-Malaysia (PAS) and the Democratic Action Party (DAP), two of the three opposition parties in the now defunct Pakatan Rakyat coalition had fallen out with each other. This led to PAS members being discouraged from attending the rally. What was more, throughout the last 18 years, the Chinese community had been slower in taking to the streets and when they finally did that in full force, it was exactly when PAS supporters were least enthusiastic.

If one wishes to, one could explain the racial pattern of participation at Bersih 4.0, to a large extent, simply as a result of inter-party conflict. What that pattern allowed though, was for its opponents to finally put a racial stamp on the movement – Bersih is a non-Malay effort!

What was more, since Bersih 4.0 was called in reaction to the recent highly dubious methods used to close options for forcing the prime minister out of power, the low participation of Malays seemed to offer Mr Najib's supporters a way to present public disapproval of him as something racially informed.

This attempt caused much confusion. There are at least two reasons for this. Firstly, Bersih 4.0 had showcased all the inclusive symbols of nationalism and patriotism its supporters could think of in order to enhance its demands for clean governance and apparently, the Malay participation was not negligible at all. Secondly, the events that had led to the present crisis of governance all had to do with suspicious electoral practices and financial maladministration.

Calls for Mr Najib's resignation have for months been coming from the UMNO leadership and from Malay leaders in general, as much as they had from non-Malay Malaysians and even foreigners. The dissatisfaction with the administration is therefore widespread, cutting across many boundaries.

As things look now, the attempt to racialise public demands for Najib to step down has been too palpably ungrounded to work.

13

One Country's Merdeka is Another's Damage Control*

It takes two hands to clap; there is no shore unless there is sea; and one man's ceiling is another man's floor, as the poet rightly claims.

You get the point. There is always a bigger picture, and that bigger picture always changes the picture, as it were. More key players are always involved, more historical trends are always being played out; and more overlapping and contesting agendas are at play than meets the eye.

It is like piecing together a puzzle. To gain a fuller insight into Malaysia's attainment of independence, we need to view the adjacent pieces as well. And the piece that cannot be ignored is the one involving the retreating colonial masters, the British.

On one side, we have the chain of interwoven events known to all Malaysian schoolchildren, which led to Merdeka. Tunku Abdul Rahman shouting 'Merdeka' seven times at the stadium in Kuala Lumpur on 31 August 1957 was in orchestration reminiscent of Mao Zedong screaming 'The Chinese people are finally back on their feet!' eight years earlier at Tiananmen Square in Beijing; and to be sure, of many other such ceremonies where national independence and liberation were declared.

But such were the times. The 1940s, 1950s and 1960s were an era when nation states sprouted into being like mushrooms all over Africa

---

* *Penang Monthly*, October 2015. (Also published in *Digital Edge Weekly*, 31 August 2015 as 'Merdeka – Unfinished Liberation').

and Asia. What this excess of cases in so short a time has meant is that the uniqueness of each case, and the legacy and lasting significance of the conditions configuring the post-colonial system of government particular to each country, tended to be disregarded. Yet, it is these conditions that have to be considered if we are to understand the now half-century or so in the history of each of these countries and if we are to identify the elements particular to each case, which have been leaving the most lasting impact.

On the other side, we have the British withdrawal to wonder about. This closing down of empire was a pan-global one and the sun would soon never rise again on the British Empire, let alone set on it. The First World War and Second World War had been fought within a span of three short decades and although the British emerged victorious, the costs were such that the Empire could not hope to win the ensuing peace.

This insight that the empire would not hold and would in fact crumble very quickly is the factor that needs to be properly studied. The decimation of British soldiers in the ditches of Western Europe between 1914 and 1918 denied the Empire a whole generation of servicemen.

The decades to follow saw Germany rise again and this time in alliance with Japan, the rising empire in the East and until recently, Britain's ally. The Second World War saw Britain under siege and it could hardly have imagined resisting in any sustained manner the onslaught of the Japanese on its Southeast Asian colonies. The port of Penang was simply abandoned, while the fortress of Singapore fell surprisingly easily.

While the British could return to their colonies in 1945 without facing armed resistance from their colonial subjects, their fellow colonialists in Indo-China and Indonesia could not. This bought them time to experiment their way towards an exit strategy that would maximise advantages, or at least the least disadvantages, to them in light of the nascent Cold War and the wildfire spread of nationalism throughout the world.

Their attempt at a starkly simplified administration in the form of the Malayan Union in 1946 quickly failed. Seen from the Malayan side, this was because it riled up the Malay elite throughout the peninsula. However, at exactly the same time, the ending of colonialism in Sumatra across the Strait of Malacca was seeing popular extreme violence being exercised on traditional leaders and the western-educated class; and by August next year, the Indian sub-continent had broken free from British rule. The violence that ensued was not something the British or anyone else wanted to see repeated anywhere else in their retreat from the East.

The chilling geopolitical situation the British now found themselves in could not but influence how they were to proceed in Malaya. The re-organisation of the Malayan administration now switched to that of a rearguard action as well as a damage control exercise. The proper transition to self-government and independence had begun – for the Malayan Union, for Singapore, for Brunei, for Sabah and for Sarawak.

The Malayan Union quickly became the Federation of Malaya. Power was principally handed back to the Malay elites and from that point on the situation of the minorities had to be negotiated from a position of weakness with UMNO and the Malay rulers.

The Malayan Communist Party reacted by taking to arms and the British hurriedly moved in to pressure Malay leaders to consider the lot of the minorities seriously for the sake of future stability and as resistance against the communist insurgency. China had just gone communist after all.

The war against the communists proceeded well after a few difficult years and the focus moved strongly to the political front. Eager to ensure stability and keep communism at bay, the British invested in conservative, read 'anti-communist', forces to be their successors.

In Malaysia, the success of the pact forged between Kuala Lumpur UMNO and Selangor MCA in the municipal election in Kuala Lumpur in February 1952 –one achieved between equals, it must be added– promised a possible way out. The Alliance was formed and it was to this coalition as victors in the elections of 1955 that leadership of the new country was awarded on 31 August 1957. In the process, however, some significant compromises were entered into, which in effect sidestepped the most serious controversies and perpetuated them as part of the fabric of Malayan politics and society.

The issue of language use remained for the future to solve, for example. More fateful were: the agreement to include religion in the otherwise secular constitution with Islam being noted as the official language; the queer decision to define ethnicity – Malayness – in the basic law of the land; and the declaration of Malay special position in that same revered document.

These would stake out the perimeters of Malaysian politics. Furthermore, by 1959, the MCA had lost any public perception of it being an equal to UMNO. In the early 1960s, the Federation of Malaya became the pillar upon which the British could pull out from the rest of its territories in the region. Malaysia was formed in 1963 and the vanity of that project was seen in Singapore's separation from the rest in 1965. Sarawak and Sabah remained in the federation and their situation would become hot issues in later decades.

The devaluation of the British pound soon followed, which along with the federal government's gradual withdrawal of Penang's free port status, led to rioting in that northern state. By the way, Penang and Malacca being combined with the rest of the peninsula in 1946 was another contingent move by the disoriented returning British colonialists.

Inter-ethnic rioting took place in 1969, following serious controversies being hotly debated in the electoral campaign of that year. When parliament was reinstated in early 1971, exactly these controversies were banned for forevermore from public and parliamentary discussion.

Another curiosity in this story is how both Malaysia and Singapore, despite their basically Westminster parliamentary system, are the countries where the ruling parties – the parties that succeeded the British – presently hold the world record for being in power the longest time.

Much of the credit for this must go to the enviable way in which the British, no doubt in response in exigencies of the time, managed the hasty dismantling of their basically mercantilist empire to their advantage.

14

Malaysia – Where Politics Must Be Ethnically Inclusive and Exclusive at the Same Time*

What any Malaysian knows at heart is that the Malay community will always dominate the politics of the country. This means in concrete terms that Malaysia's key leaders will always nominally and in reality be Malay Muslims.

However, the country's population is a very mixed one and from the very beginning, leaders of the Malay community who wish to be remembered as statesmen and respected as nation builders have had to expound the idea that Malay interests do not necessarily contradict national interest or even the interests of other communities.

UMNO's first president famously tried to change the party's name from United Malay National Organisation to United Malayan National Organisation. He realised what most of his followers had not yet realised. Malaysian politics has to be multi-ethnically sensitive.

His successor as UMNO president, Tunku Abdul Rahman Putra, would realise this. Under him, UMNO grew from strength to strength based on the slogan of 'Merdeka' rather than 'Hidup Melayu'; the latter having been the raison d'etre of the Malay party since its founding. More importantly, teaming up with the Malayan Chinese Association in 1952 made his party's agenda more clearly an inclusive one. And with

---

* *The Edge*, Malaysia, 26 October 2015.

that move, broad support could be gained and Merdeka was gained at an earlier time than expected.

As truly as Malay dominance is an inescapable reality for Malaysia, a central policy direction that is ethnically inclusive is unavoidable for sufficient harmony to be achieved so that its economy can gain the trust of both domestic and international investors, and grow to its full potential.

Ethnic tensions saw riots breaking out in 1969. The Tunku had to retire and his successors put into place powerful constitutional curbs on the freedom of speech in the public sphere and in parliament. Other measures were taken for UMNO to secure a stronger hold on power in its proclaimed role as the champion of Malay collective interests. But before the next general elections could be called, the new prime minister Tun Abdul Razak Hussein had made certain that the ruling coalition would now include as many parties representing as possible. To top it off, he arranged for a much publicised visit by him to China to begin Malaysia's normalisation of ties with the communist giant.

This saw him winning a convincing victory in the 1974 general elections – quite an achievement considering how divided the country was in 1969.

Now, let's move forward to the late 1980s when UMNO was in deep trouble and Prime Minister Mahathir Mohamad was seriously challenged from within the party by Tengku Razaleigh Hamzah. Mahathir survived as party president, and as prime minister, he used the Internal Security Act on critics at this time and purportedly averted what might have been another racial conflict in the country. The New Economic Policy, a comprehensive affirmative action policy started in 1970 in favour of the Malay community, was also coming to its official end and a replacement for it that was acceptable to all communities was not constructed yet.

And so, Mahathir did badly in the 1990 general elections. But with a stroke of genius, he came up with the idea of Bangsa Malaysia and Vision 2020 the following year. Helped by steady global economic growth, he became a very popular prime minister for the next seven years until the Asian financial crisis of 1997–98 opened up a deep irreparable schism between him and his deputy, Anwar Ibrahim.

What was so effective about Bangsa Malaysia was of course that it was Mahathir's version and vision of inclusive development for the country's various communities. Vision 2020 spelt out the evolution of Malaysians who have discarded his fixation with race and who have grown confident and modern because they have become educated and knowledgeable about the world at large.

The confrontation between the two top leaders of UMNO at this time also reflected and exacerbated differences within the Malay community which were ideological and which had socio-economic basis. The Malays were becoming an increasingly diverse community – largely due to the success of many of the Malay-centric policies of the previous decades.

Probably seeing that he had become a strongly polarising figure, especially among the Malays, Mahathir retired, handing the leadership over to someone whose character promised to have a more healing effect on the population. This was Abdullah Badawi. As an inclusive kind of leader whose public agenda was to reform the country's governance and limit the damage done by Mahathir's excesses, Abdullah managed to garner enough votes to give his coalition a record number of seats in parliament in 2004.

The lesson learned so far is this. Malaysia's top leader must always be a Malay who styles himself as the champion of Malay interests. But to succeed well as a nation builder, he must at the same time inject an inclusive agenda into his discourse and policies.

Under Abdullah, however, excessive displays of Malay-centrism followed his electoral triumph. Cases of Muslim authorities snatching bodies of purported Muslim converts away from their non-Muslim funeral, the dismantling of Indian temples and the unsheathing and raising of the Malay keris at UMNO annual assemblies infected the social ambience most negatively. This divisiveness was made plain in the 2008 general elections when the Barisan Nasional lost five states and the two-thirds majority in parliament that it had become used to having.

And so, Abdullah had to be replaced. In April 2009, Najib Razak took over. His job was to win back the votes that had been lost. He began by adopting the slogan 'One Malaysia'. This was of course meant to express the inclusiveness that all UMNO leaders, however ethnocentric, have had to adopt in order to be an effective prime minister.

Despite programmes for transforming the government and the economy, Najib never succeeded in gaining broad support for his discourse. The contradictions were simply too many, and also, by the time he took the stage, the game had congealed into a two-party battle and the new media had severely undermined the mainstream media that had been a mainstay of BN power.

In pandering to UMNO's right wing for fear of losing that final bastion of support, Najib ended up losing not only the chance to regain non-Malay sympathy, but also the Malay middle ground.

The paradox of Malaysian politics is thus this: Malay exclusivity cannot be taken too far. This is because Malaysia is a multi-ethnic country whichever way one looks at it. Today, BN relies more than ever on support from East Malaysia, which makes multi-ethnicity an even more important inherent characteristic of Malaysia to recognise.

15

Is Malaysia at a Crossroads or in a Quagmire?*

Malaysia has drawn the attention of the global community in recent times and this has largely been much more as negative publicity than positive. Just last Thursday, the European Parliament passed a resolution deploring 'the deteriorating human rights situation in Malaysia and in particular the crackdown on civil society activists, academics, media and political activists.'

This follows a series of reports throughout the year in the Wall Street Journal on scandals in high places in Malaysia. These are just two of many other cases.

While this sustained attention from abroad is new, the analysis tends to be too much focused on the contemporariness conditions than it should be. Malaysians in general understand the country's difficult situation to be a profound one, rooted in a unique history as much as in notional narrowness.

The country may have gained independence in a relatively easy manner, but over time, no one should have thought that the nation-building to come would be an easy one. Many things have changed but the question remains: Is Malaysia a country at a crossroads or in a quagmire?

That is as relevant a question today to ask about Malaysia as it ever has been. I am more prone than ever to ask it though after reading

---

* *The Edge*, Malaysia, 28 December 2015.

some books very recently about the social history and politics of the late colonial period in British Malaya.

Throughout the 1930s, Malay newspapers were being established to satisfy the growing need among Malay intellectuals to discuss the situation of their community. The world was in a deep economic crisis then and the growing notions of nationhood and ethnic essentialism led to a hostile debate between those professing the term 'Malayans' and those Malays who would not recognise that notion. The Malay newspapers were those driving the debate most consistently.

More than 80 years later, from the vantage point of 2015 going into 2016, it is stimulating to compare the two periods and to see what has changed and what has stubbornly remained the same.

This article cannot profess to give a list of these things; it can only prod readers to proceed on their own and study and contemplate the exciting history of late colonialism in order to better understand the Malaysian nation, as it stands today.

The underlying contradiction between Melayu and Malayan continues to infect the debate today, though robed in other terms. The essential twain refuse to meet. In fact, it has expanded to become about the gap between Bumiputera and Malaysian.

With the peoples of East Malaysia added to the equation and the use of Islam to incorporate Muslims of Arabic and Indian descent into the Melayu denomination, racial politics has become a very complex game to manage.

This polarity remains the larger framework within which Malaysian politics is played.

One other similarity is that the country is in economic crisis, at least at the people level if not at the GDP level. It is common for people under economic stress to be susceptible to the machinations of opportunists playing on ethnic and religious sentiments. And we see such opportunists a-plenty today.

The key difference of course is that Malaysia is over half a century old. The British are long gone and although the handover of power to Malayan leaders was done to favour conservative power structures, national politics have taken over from colonial politics. The national economy has replaced the colonial economy. But to what extent has the colonial and colonised mindset been dropped? Do Malaysians still fight battles of yore whatever the cost to future prospects for their children?

Fifty years of nation-building and of five-year plans must surely have improved the prospects for healthier inter-ethnic relations and diversified the collective identification of individual Malaysians, even if news reports tell us differently.

The greatest change in recent times, to my mind, has been taking place within the Malay community. The Malay population is now large enough, urbanised enough, educated enough, young enough and exposed enough to the world to rethink the country's demographic, historical and global situation for themselves.

It is hard to refute the argument that all major changes in the country must involve the Malay community.

Most people will have discerned a growing demand in Malaysia from all communities for good governance in the country over the last two decades. Despite heightened inter-ethnic tensions, the discourse has definitely diversified. Many of the political challenges that the country is facing signal that it is at a crossroads.

What's more, the regionalising of Asia tends to weaken the fixation with domestic politics that plague all new nations. This should increasingly force political considerations to adopt the region as the proper framework within which to formulate effective policies. So even if Malaysia is in a quagmire, the means for it to pull itself out are many.

And so, back to the original question: Crossroads or Quagmire? The answer has to be: it is up to the people themselves to decide through future actions how decisive they want their historical condition to be. It is also possible for them to rise to the occasion and not be stuck in shortsighted defensiveness.

16

Unity Without Solidarity Sows Disunity*

The biggest parade in Malaysian political narrative is how the call for unity is in reality a call for disunity. This comes about because calls for unity tend to be rhetorical appeals for racial unity vis-à-vis other races.

Since all societies today, and Malaysia started out already that way, are multi-cultural in reality, racial unity means inter-racial disunity. Such a paradigm cannot help but incessantly provoke confrontation and distrust. No common long-term goals can be sustained. Worse than that, any serious discussion becomes potentially a polarising one, be it over type of education, form of worship, style of dressing, food for eating, treatment of women, etc.

As the distrust grows, the calls for unity take on a religious character – religion being the major historical determinant of race. We see this happen more and more the worse the country's economic conditions become. This is nothing new, nothing surprising.

We saw how desperate times in Germany in the 1930s led to the rise of a radically racist regime and the momentum of that change quickly led to the destruction of traditional German society. With the fall of Adolf Hitler's Third Reich in 1945, it became politically inexcusable in the West to use 'race' as the rationale for formulating policies. In academia, we saw the dropping of the term 'race' from practically all discussions, in favour of 'ethnicity' as the apparently more neutral and therefore more scientifically acceptable concept.

---

* *The Edge*, Malaysia, 28 December 2015.

Racialism became a rhetorical taboo globally. This did not in any way mean that racism was history. Far from it. It just meant that policy arguments based on race had very little traction after the Second World War. There were still some attempts to plant racialism as the rationale for state building. One was the generally unrecognised Republic of Rhodesia, which in 1978 had to transform itself into multicultural Zimbabwe. Another more significant case was South Africa's apartheid regime, which lasted too long – from 1948 to 1994.

In the USA, where the suppression of black Americans had continued despite the ending of slavery in 1865, the civil rights movement managed in the 1960s to reduce substantially racial bias in administrative practices.

I am not claiming that racialism in Malaysia will necessarily bring doom, but it certainly does not bode well and it does not promise anything positive in the long run for the country as a whole. Pre-war Europe is not post-war Southeast Asia. Malaysia is not Germany.

And yet, while the West was fighting wars partially caused by the logic of ethno-nationalism, all over the colonised world, new countries came into being for whom 'nationalism' was a rallying cry – and a very positive term. Its potency lay in it being a conceptual antidote to colonialism; to control by external powers.

The situation was always a complicated one. The construction of states from colonies, the transformation of colonial sub-economies into national ones and the uniting of diverse ethnicities into a nationality; all this did not happen in a vacuum.

The Malay community, in their first show of unity, rejected the Malayan Union in 1946 as an attempt by the British to finally colonise them thoroughly. This jarred starkly with the view in the eyes of the world that the workings of British colonial manipulation over a century and more had in effect already incorporated Malay livelihoods into the global economy that was run from London. In fact, for all the Malayan communities, political life at this time was very much secondary to economic survival.

Given the plural society from which Malaysia emerged, late colonialism's inter-ethnic disparity and inter-cultural dissonance bred a consciousness of Us versus Them; of the local, the bumiputera, the

Melayu on one side, versus the extra-regional, the pendatang and the colonially imported peoples on the other side. And so, it appears totally natural today that Malaysian politics should be as racialised as it is.

Yet, this development was far from being a given thing. A development based on class consciousness alongside, if not above, ethnic consciousness was always in the offing. And this was most poignant if one focused on the Malay community itself. Arrayed against the so-called conservative alternative that the British fully supported for fear of violent anti-colonialism and anti-monarchism from the masses were Malays who sought a post-colonial system that was more people-based, who highlighted solidarity with the poor and who prioritised the eradication of poverty.

The latter lost out, as we know. But what requires revisiting today is the fact that the race-based system, which preserved the status quo of power where the Malay community was concerned, relies on unity through racial sentiments, then, now and in the future. It unites by dissociating one ethnicity from the others; and by propagating the false idea that any other alternative would be insidiously detrimental to Malay progress.

What unity through racial sentiments has done is to cause policymakers to ignore the sufferings of the less privileged from all ethnic groups and kept politicians in office whose power base is divisiveness. Unity through racialism is a very effective way of perpetuating national disunity. Sadly, it seems to be a durable solution as well.

17

UMNO and Looking Back at History*

This year, 2016, is a special year for Malaysia. This is not because of the Sarawak state elections due in April (according to some sources); not because of the alarming economic situation facing so many already poor Malaysians today; nor is it because of the risk of a terrorist attack being foretold by external sources that are generally not given to be being alarmist. Neither is it because of the general reputation of the country hitting a new low following internationally noted scandals involving the prime minister.

The year is historical because UMNO, the party that has ruled the country since independence in 1957 and that has been the one to decide the direction of Malaysia's political thought for 60 years turns 70 years old.

The United Malays National Organisation is the result of a broad and passionate reaction to the Malayan Union – a post-war British policy that Malays saw as a move to colonise Malaya for good. What this turn of events also showed was how for over a century, the Malay community at large seemed to have strangely considered British control over most of the peninsula to be anything less than colonisation. In truth, British colonialism was often about economic control more than about direct exercise of power.

Importantly, colonial economics was a global phenomenon that involved the migration of peoples within the British sphere of

---

* *The Edge*, Malaysia, 7 March 2016.

influence. In the case of Malaya, colonialism started out with the securing of ports to create a trading route stretching from the Chinese coast all the way back to Europe. Over time and with the growth of the tin and rubber industries on the peninsula itself, the peninsula became a land of plantations and mines.

Peoples were moved as a policy to support these industries or they migrated voluntarily for work. And they came from far away, aided by the maritime infrastructure already in place. This resettling of people was essential to the growth of the colonial economy.

All this is part and parcel of the globalisation of the world over the last 500 years. The pretence kept up for seven decades by Malay rulers and the elite in concurrence with British strategies, limited their subjects involvement in globalising processes.

With increased political consciousness around the time of the Second World War and the rise of Malay literacy came the realisation in the community, debated strongly in the 1950s through Utusan Melayu, that there was indeed a huge gap between the knowledge, political and economic challenges of the time and what the Malay community in general was prepared for. The enormity of this challenge for the Malays was all the more obvious when their situation was compared to that of non-Malay residents, who had from *the* start been involved in some way or other with the global economy, even if at the very bottom of the ladder.

Malaya's territories had in economic and other terms been colonised, and the rejection of the Malayan Union was not a rejection of colonialism and its globalising ambitions. It was too late for that. It was an expression of the myth that Malaya was not a colony.

One can therefore see why the need for Malay unity was so strongly felt in the period immediately following the war. Coming into being in such an emotive atmosphere, UMNO's members found it hard to go beyond the original motivation for the party. The myth continued, and even the party founder, the hugely popular Onn Ja'afar, could not do much about it. From his perch, he could sense that for the party to lead Malayan society in its entirety, it needed to accept the fact that post-colonial Malaya could not be the same as pre-colonial Malaya. Colonialism had already happened and the demographic, economic and political influences it brought had already changed the Malay world – not to mention the whole world.

But Onn Ja'afar failed to push his party beyond the ethnocentric mode in which it was founded. It is as strategy that Onn Ja'afar's vehement push to open up the party to non-Malays can be seen to be ahead of his time. In fact, it should be seen as the perspective that one would expect of someone with his exposure, position and calibre to have. For a fleeting moment, he perceived the Malayan population as a multicultural entity configured and fused over decades by the political economy of colonialism and not simply as a purely Malay one recently awakened to the approach of colonisation.

The idea that Malayan society was essentially a Malay one that had played – and was playing – host to visiting non-Malays on their territory would triumph within UMNO after Onn Ja'afar. The country's multicultural reality was managed and sidestepped through the Alliance model. This model consisted of parties each representing a race, to form a coalition, thus intrinsically keeping the communities apart.

Onn Ja'afar's successor, Tunku Abdul Rahman, was liberal enough person but he soon had to give way to others who advocated Malay ethnocentrism much more fervently than he did.

Now, 60 years after the Alliance came to power, UMNO politics – cocooned with the Barisan Nasional coalition – continues to deny Malaysia's multicultural society that the political economy of British colonialism had created.

What makes matters worse today is that UMNO has chosen to exploit the Muslimness and religiosity of the Malays to control that constituency and to divide it further from others. Significantly, this happens at the same time that Malays have clearly become too diverse to be represented by the simple notion of Malay ethnocentrism.

Now 70 years old, UMNO is increasingly feeling the pressure to step back into its past and to recognise the fact that the Malay Peninsula was effectively colonised long before the Malayan Union project was implemented and that its population has been multicultural for 200 years.

18

Sarawak Forces Federal Opposition to Do Deep Soul-searching. But Can it?*

Practically all pundits predicted that the Barisan Nasional (BN) in Sarawak, headed by the PBB under the leadership of Chief Minister Adenan Satem, would win big in the Sarawak state election held last Saturday, 7 May. They were right, no surprises there.

What was surprising was how many fronts the Sarawak BN won on. It took the coveted two-thirds majority, in fact winning 72 of 82 seats; its share of the popular vote went up to almost 62 per cent from 55 per cent in 2011; the introduction of direct BN candidates succeeded as well, diffusing tensions within the coalition; and its Chinese-based party, the SUPP, came out looking like it still has a future, unlike the Chinese-based BN parties on the peninsula.

Following any election, the figures tend to get heavily over-analysed and comparisons back in time tend to forget that apples have sometimes along the way become oranges. It is instead the broader trends that need to be noted.

Firstly, this election is very much a Sarawak election and what has been happening in the last decade is that in light of the weakened situation of the BN at the federal level, the uniqueness of Sarawak state has become politically prominent and salient.

---

* *The Edge*, Malaysia, 16 May 2016.

Sarawak has its own profound provincial politics, its own self-image ('othered' often vis-à-vis West Malaysia) and its own special mix of multiculturalism. All these cannot be subsumed under and analysed with categories generated in West Malaysia the way politicians and pundits from the peninsula wish to do.

It is in fact through portraying Sarawakian exceptionalism well in policy and public statements that made Adenan the unquestioned man of the hour. His assertion that he just wants one more term to finish what he started – and given his health, few doubt this to be other than sincerely stated – went down well with the population. Since he had clearly over the last two years as Chief Minister been mending fences among Sarawak's diverse communities (in stark contrast to the opposite tendency manifesting on the peninsula under the UMNO-led BN there) and pressing for increased autonomy for Sarawak in public discourses – and as a clear of success on these fronts have had the Prime Minister Najib Razak endlessly calling on and courting the Sarawak state government– there is little reason for most Sarawakians not to allow him a strong mandate for a few more years.

Secondly, the re-delineation exercise in Sarawak, which created 11 new constituencies favoured the incumbent coalition, as such exercises tend to do. This, together with other measures that only the incumbent can undertake, such as banning key opposition politicians from the peninsula from entering and campaigning, tweaking the extremely difficult logistics involved in campaigning in Sarawak in favour of BN candidates; as well as disburse huge sums of money in dubious ways, made for a very uneven playing field.

Looking at the results, much of this tweaking seems to be overkill. A lot of the bullying seems unnecessary now and does taint the victory for Adenan. He would have won handsomely in any case, based on the popularity he accrued as a leader and on the moral capital he had collected. But the lethargy of change within any complex system is always strong. Much of how things were done, continues to be how things are done. And political culture is one of the hardest things to change.

Thirdly, Sarawak exceptionalism, a sentiment that the opposition parties had fanned in recent years as a strategic move to weaken the BN, seems now to have worked against them. Today, the Sarawakian government knows it can control the federal government's influence in Sarawak much better than it can control the opposition.

Sarawak exceptionalism would therefore require that the latter be effectively curbed. After all, the federal government comes a-courting while the opposition comes a-challenging. There are definitely painful lessons in strategy to be learned here for the opposition parties as they now withdraw to lick their wounds. And these considerations should go beyond simple electoral campaigning mistakes.

The options that were open to the incumbent in Sarawak should not have – and would not have – come as a surprise to them. The opposition was really hoping against hope in any case.

In truth, the next big battle, which is the general election due by mid-2018, requires a re-focus by the opposition on two major points, if they are to have even a small chance at winning. The first concerns their failure to rule in exemplary fashion in the states that they have controlled since 2008 and the second is the failure to develop a national discourse that goes beyond broad principles, towards integrated policies that express good governance.

By 'rule in exemplary fashion', I mean that the newly entrenched ruling parties' interlocutions with their constituents must be genuine, structured and allowed to mature; and that the quality of their power holders at all levels must improve so as to replace patronage practices with meritocratic ones. Without these, convincing a rightly sceptical electorate to move in sufficient numbers to defeat a sitting long-term federal government at the ballot box is quixotic.

The two major points mentioned above are interlinked. Having power at the state level allows not only for policy thinking to be based on genuine public consultation but for resultant sound policies to be showcased. This was the process through which the Reformasi discourse should have since 2008 developed into concrete and integrated ideas for raising the level of governance in a concrete and evident manner.

Considerations of these points are necessary. Otherwise, more fiascos await the opposition.

19

By-elections Reveal New Malay Politics*

On 5 May, in the midst of the Sarawak state election campaign, a helicopter crashed in the jungle and killed five people, including the Malaysian Deputy Minister for Plantation Industries and Commodities, Datuk Noriah Kasnon and the Member of Parliament for Kuala Kangsar, Sundaran Annamalai.

This means that the political acrimony that elections whip up will persist for a while yet since two simultaneous by-elections will now have to be held. This is not to say that the Malaysian political scene needs any help in staying rancorous.

The by-elections – in Kuala Kangsar in Perak state and in Sungei Besar in Selangor – are scheduled for 18 June; but while technically minor battles, they are part of bigger political wars being fought in Malaysia at the same time.

These conflicts were adequately demonstrated on 17 May when Anwar Ibrahim, the jailed leader of Parti Keadilan Rakyat (PKR) and unofficial opposition leader, issued an eight-page letter to his followers to exercise caution and wisdom in following the lead of his long-time nemesis, former Prime Minister Mahathir Mohamad, in the latter's attempt to unseat Prime Minister Najib Razak through signed support from over a million Malaysians. Many from the opposition and from civil society groups have indeed given open support for Mahathir's

---

* *The Straits Times*, Singapore, 26 May 2016.

Citizens' Declaration, helping it to go already beyond the million-signature target.

In essence, the key points of Anwar's letter were firstly a pronouncement that he 'is inclined not to be seen to be uniting with the Citizen's Declaration group, and to start to set a distance'; and secondly to state that the Declaration was 'Tun M's document, effective and incoherent viewed in the context of reform'. The distrust between the two men is obvious and understandable but there is also fear of Mahathir effectively usurping the role of opposition leader.

Beyond the noise, these events send out obstinate signals that tell us something profound about Malaysia's present socio-political situation.

Only diehards now imagine that significantly more non-Malay support for the opposition than it so impressively garnered in the 2013 elections is forthcoming. In the recent Sarawak state election, it was the Democratic Action Party – a basically Chinese party that is trying to be re-recognised as a multiracial one – that was the main loser. It had been hoping to show that it could win votes from Sarawak's diverse communities but instead it fared dismally in failing to maintain the increments in support from the Chinese and the indigenous peoples that it had enjoyed for at least three successive elections.

This, among other developments, should lead us to reconsider the present political landscape of the country. What we have been seeing in the last two decades – perhaps since the fallout between Mahathir and Anwar in 1998 – is persistent socio-political diversification in the Malay community. This is expressed in the founding of at least two new Malay-based parties, in the fervent establishment of Malay-language magazines, newspapers and publishers and in the apparent crisis in Malay leadership. And that is not considering the rise of social media and web news sites.

In this context, the coming by-elections carry great significance. The DAP already realises that its role can only be supportive because these are Malay majority seats. What becomes manifest then – and this reflects the larger national picture – is that these battles will be totally between Malay-based parties and between Malay personalities.

The results of these by-elections promise therefore insight into how the Malay ground in the key states of Selangor and Perak has been affected since the 2013 general elections by Premier Najib's turn to the right, by the many scandals involving him, by the top-level strife within the all-powerful United Malays National Organisation (UMNO), by the breakup of the opposition Pakatan Rakyat coalition, by the split in Parti Islam SeMalaysia (PAS) which led to the formation of the more progressive Parti Amanah Negara, by the second jailing of Anwar Ibrahim and by Mahathir Mohamad's Citizen's Declaration, which has seen him performing more and more like the opposition leader.

And most importantly, they can give an indication of how the political sentiments of rural and semi-urban Malays have been affected by their economic travails of recent months; and how much of these will be blamed on the implementation of the GST and the government's general mismanagement of the economy.

PAS, which lost narrowly in 2013 to UMNO both in Kuala Kangsar, where the Malays make up 68 per cent of the population, and in Sungai Besar and which is now without official coalitional ties, wants to contest against UMNO again in both cases. Amanah, its breakaway party, sees a chance here to test its potential for the first time since its recent founding and may be willing to compromise and concentrate on one seat and leave the other to PAS. But even that is not certain as yet. And Anwar's PKR, which runs Selangor state, may not be too willing to play merely a supporting role in Sungai Besar.

Mahathir in turn has surprised everyone by taking the liberty to call on the opposition parties to avoid three-corner fights and to focus on the task at hand – which is to defeat his own former party, UMNO. He had in nearly April, astounded many by calling for 'foreign interference' to oust Najib. His latest statement, however, had him sounding like a self-appointed leader of the opposition and this may have precipitated Anwar's eight-pager to his followers.

What may have forced Mahathir's hand could be the concern that he should now have that Premier Najib, buoyed as he already is by Barisan Nasional's landslide in Sarawak, may be intensely tempted to call for snap general elections should the BN win the by-elections with strong margins.

A bad show by both Pakatan Harapan (represented by Amanah) and by PAS in the coming by-elections would confirm voter disenchantment with the opposition and with their agenda for change and that would convince Najib that a snap election is to be preferred.

Should he then lead the BN to a new federal mandate, and if that turns out furthermore to be a stronger one than what he had in 2013, then any hope by his detractors to remove him would be buried.

20

Interview with Mahathir Mohamad: 'People Must Be Able to Hold Their Heads Up'*

Tun Dr Mahathir Mohamad was in Penang as part of his cross-country tour, and as a guest of Penang Institute, to gather at least one million signatures for the Citizen's Declaration he initiated. He spent 20 minutes talking with Ooi Kee Beng in between arriving from KL with Tun Dr Siti Hasmah and rushing off to deliver his speech at the packed Straits Quay Convention Centre. The interview took place in the late afternoon on 8 May 2016 at the E&O Hotel.

* * *

Dr Ooi Kee Beng: Tun, your generation fascinates me. You are of the nation-building generation who dared to imagine that it would not only change the world, but configure it to fit local conditions. The impact of that generation has of course been enormous in all post-colonial countries but that generation is passing. What advice would you give young Malaysians about the future, given what you see now of global economic dynamics and the political situation in Malaysia today?

Tun Dr Mahathir Mohamad: The first thing for people to learn is the history of the country because if you don't have an understanding of the background of the country, you cannot make an assessment of events or of the improvements that have taken place. Many Malaysians today were born long after Independence. I would tell them that what we are seeing today is completely different from what we had under

---

* *Penang Monthly*, June 2016.

the British or even in the early days of Independence. So we must be able to make a comparison between the past and the present.

OKB: If there is one word to describe you, Tun, I would use the word 'nationalist'. You are very much, for want of a better word, a situationalist. Your analysis of events and different times shifts as things evolve; you seem very tuned into evolving dynamics. In that sense the methods you adopt would be understood best in a tactical mode. Would that be correct?

MM: I was trained as a doctor and a doctor approaches a problem with a certain method. He has to know the background, the history of the patient and do an additional examination to see what the problem is. For a sick person or for a community, it is the same thing. Once you adopt that approach, you recognise a problem much more clearly. And after recognising what the problem is, you can think about how to resolve it. Having been trained as a doctor, I approach most problems that way. I find it to be really very easy. It is methodical and it is very consistent and often quite accurate.

You may end up with three possibilities, for example, and then you will have to do a further analysis to determine which disease it really is and what the cure should be. It is the same with a community –you have to determine what the problem is first.

OKB: But are there shortcomings to that kind of approach?

MM: Well, I suppose there are. There are of course people who can instinctively see what the problem is and come up with a solution. But instinct is not methodical. It may come or it may not come. You have no control over it. But the methodical process of examination by doctors is something that you do almost automatically and you eliminate other possibilities to arrive at the right diagnosis.

OKB: One has to always consider multiple factors.

MM: Yes.

OKB: Since you have been in the limelight for an amazingly long time – in fact since after the Second World War, when you started writing as Che Det – you are very overexposed by now and one would expect people who are overexposed to be very predictable. Yet you are not. You can be very unpredictable. I tend to think that when people are unpredictable, it is usually because they are being misunderstood. People have their own logic and in following that logic, they are really being consistent.

I would like to ask you a straightforward and personal question: 'What motivates you deep down?' How do we see consistency and how do we make sense of your actions over the last 70 years? You do know that many think that you are often contradictory.

MM: Like you said earlier, I am a nationalist. That's what motivates me. I have been exposed to many things inside the country and outside the country. The desire to do things, to achieve and to be proud of what [I] can do... [that] is consistent. You just have to do something to improve any situation. The situation may be already good, but you have to think – what else can you do?

So in that sense, there is consistency all the time. When I was a young boy, I saw poverty; I saw people who were jobless and living very poor lives. I felt it was not right. You see that some people are rich and some people are very poor and some people do not even have regular meals. These are social problems and when you see problems like that, you want to do something. We are brought up that way, to be concerned about people who are less fortunate than we are. So if they are less fortunate, what do we do for them?

Throughout my career that has been my motivation and even the approach has been very consistent. I don't come up suddenly with some fantastic thing. I think things over to myself. For example, when I wanted to resign [as Prime Minister in 2003], I did not tell anybody. I thought it was time for me to resign and give place to others. So without anybody pushing me out, I resigned.

OKB: I suppose the poor usually can't help themselves and so those who have the opportunity have the responsibility to help them.

MM: That is true of course. The rich get richer, the poor get poorer – at least relatively speaking. The rich can get richer because they have the means. For example, in business, they have the capital and if they see an opportunity, they make use of that opportunity to enrich themselves. A poor man may see an opportunity but he has no capital, so he will forever be poor because he does not have the means. So what we should do is not only give him the opportunity but also give him the means to make use of that opportunity.

OKB: You are practically a socialist, are you not?

MM: Socialism itself is not bad. But it is sometimes used to oppress people and that is bad. A system is good only if you make use of it properly. During colonial times, the Europeans were the 'masters'. You called them 'Tuan', and you think that they are superior and that they know a lot while you don't. And they can do what you cannot do. And in a way, you feel very inferior. You get an inferiority complex.

OKB: The whole of society, really…

MM: Yes. I asked myself, am I as inferior as they make it out to be? Well, I thought, they are there because of their dominance over the people. They have practically colonised the country and they are given [good] jobs, authority and power. That was what made them superior people. They could do what you could not do.

OKB: These experiences in your younger days must have affected you very deeply.

MM: Yes, very much. But I was fortunate. I was among the 20 or so boys who had the opportunity to go to an English school. There were hundreds of others who were equally good, but they did not get the opportunity to get a good education. It seemed to me quite unfair.

You had the opportunity, they didn't have the opportunity. So, the solution to that is to create the opportunity and to give them the means to make use of the opportunity for their own good.

OKB: Being one of the few privileged ones, you felt this to be your responsibility then?

MM: Yes.

OKB: One of the great innovations of your time was Vision 2020. If I ask you to reformulate Vision 2020 today, would there be things in there that would be different from before?

MM: We wanted to be a developed country but a developed country in our own mould, not just a copy of some other developed country. So we started spelling out what we meant by 'in our own mould'. What do you mean by being developed?

If we do not define it properly, people tend to take the simple definition, which is that if you have money then you are developed.

So you see the stress on per capita income. If you have a per capita income of [US$] 15,000 or 30,000, then you are developed.

But that is not true. I have always thought that thinking in averages is a very bad way of assessing anything. I tell people that they can drown in a river with an average depth of two feet. If one man is a millionaire and 999 men are poverty-stricken then the average [wealth] is $1000. You see, averages are not a very good measurement of achievements.

So you have to define what you mean by development. And to me, it is not just about per capita income. It is about our capacity. Do we have very well-educated people? Do we do research and development? Do we produce things by ourselves? Are we industrialised? All these things must be there before you can consider yourself developed. At the moment, the stress is far too much on per capita income. Per capita is an average and it is not a good measurement.

OKB: It's more about people's integrity and dignity, isn't it?

MM: Yeah! People must be able to hold their heads up, to stand tall like other people.

OKB: Something that would have happened along the way since the 1990s would be the development of 'Melayu Baru', the New Malay. It's a new world today and the Malays are in a different place as a community and also in their relationship with other communities. Are we seeing something that you would have foreseen, that once the Malays reached a certain level of development a lot of conflict would also come into play?

MM: I spent a lot of time when I was Prime Minister to try and change the value system and the culture of the Malays because I believe it is the value system that determines if you do well or not. I must admit that I wasn't very successful. But a few of them have acquired new values, new ways of thinking. We do see quite a number of Malay professionals and Malay businessmen who do well. But the rest are not doing so well.

This can be corrected if you can change their mindset.

OKB: You just need to go to the next stage... But do you then think that things are going backwards? I suppose you do.

MM: Now, the focus is not on changing the culture. The focus is now on… well, giving [people] things without their earning those things. That's bad.

OKB: But people generally don't like to change or don't like to be told to change.

MM: Yes, but we change all the time.

OKB: We do.

MM: Whether we like it or not, we change. If you lived in a kampung and you move into a town, and you still want to live like you did in the kampung, that's not possible. In fact, we had a problem housing people in places like Kampung Abdullah Hukum and Kampung Kerinchi in KL. They wanted to have a house like they used to, elevated so they can rear chickens underneath, plant some vegetables around the house.

That is not possible in town. In town, you have to have high-rise buildings, you have to live in flats. And living in flats means there are adjustments to be made. You cannot grow vegetables, you cannot rear any chickens. If you don't make these adjustments, you can't really live in an urban area.

OKB: One amazing aspect of your life is that you have fought from within UMNO and you have fought from outside UMNO. And by UMNO, I am connoting mainstream politics in Malaysia, really. That has left many people confused, even pundits. It must at times get rather confusing even for you.

MM: Well, when you form a political party, you have an objective. What are you struggling for? When you are running UMNO and you forget your objective and you veer away and you go for other things, then I don't see any reason why I should be inside the party. UMNO is [supposed to be] dedicated to developing Malaysia, to ensure that people enjoy a good life, that everybody has a share of the wealth and power in this country.

But then you find that some leaders do not focus on that. They focus instead on something to make themselves happy. For example, they think that the best thing to do is to give money to people, and in that way, become popular. These are not to be found in the objectives of founding UMNO.

That's why sometimes I am in and sometimes I am out [of UMNO].

OKB: Two Malaysian Prime Ministers ruled for a substantial period of time and were very influential. These are you and Tunku Abdul Rahman. What is your appraisal of Tunku Abdul Rahman today?

MM: The Tunku contributed a lot to the country. He was the one who won independence for the country. He was also the one who solved a very difficult problem –the problem of multiracialism. Normally, in a multiracial country, there will be conflicts for different reasons. Such countries will not be stable and you cannot develop such countries. But Tunku found a way out for Malaysia. He decided that they should share this country, all these races. He came up with this idea of a coalition –not a single multiracial party because a single multiracial party doesn't work. Some have tried to have a party with multiracial membership but that didn't work because people were still not familiar with each other.

So he came up with this idea of a coalition. You remain as you are in your own party looking after your community and yet you have a common objective [with the other communities], you see? And when wealth is created, then all will have a share. Even the power. You must share the power, you must share the wealth.

So this was put into the Constitution.

OKB: I see your aides are telling us that we have to stop talking now. Let me squeeze in one last question. You are from Alor Setar, not very far away from Penang. Can you share some thoughts about Penang, your reminiscences of the place perhaps?

MM: My father came from Penang. In those days, when you wanted to go some place different, you went to Penang. Penang was a developed town. But Penang has not changed that much. Some parts are very modern. The quay and all that, they are all still the same –ramshackle buildings and all that, and not very tidy, I must say.

One part has changed, the other has remained as it was before independence. But I think this is a problem with democracy. When you want to do something that is good all round, there will be people who will object. And well, you don't want to be unpopular, so you allow these things to go on.

I think they did a better job in KL. If you go to KL, you don't see those ramshackle zinc sheds anymore.

OKB: Thank you for your time and for sharing.

21

Malaysia Has to Start Re-examining Its Histories*

When studying humanity and its history, what one does is construct a narrative. And in that narrative, one distinguishes heroes from villains, outlines territories and peoples and differentiates steady trends from turning points.

Since different choices result in different stories, it is understandable that power-holders use whatever means they can to popularise storylines that they think serve them best. That is the nature of states. But what happens when the narrative leads consistently to negative outcomes?

In the case of Malaysia where quarrelling and squabbling now pass for discussion and debate, what we are often left with are disjointed ideas about what Malaysia is, what Malaysia was, what Malaysians are and what Malaysians are supposed to become. This would seem to have resulted from the over-politicisation of the national consciousness and over a long time.

Another way to describe this is to equate the Malaysian way of doing politics with the spraying of ink by the shrewd sotong. It sprays ink to confuse more than to contest. It does not wish you to know where it is going.

The problem is, if it does this too often and for too long, the sotong becomes as lost and confused as its enemy. It too does not know

---

* *The Edge*, Malaysia, 26 June 2016.

where it is going. The contest becomes everything; it becomes its own goal, it becomes a way of life. All are locked in a futile fight where even the winner recognises that his triumph is really a loss. There are no real winners.

But how is the country to break out into a new consciousness and attain a new way for Malaysians to relate to each other? Short of having an authoritarian figure forcing his will onto the whole of society, it would seem that sustainable change has to come from young adults who wish to break the tortuous trap in which the country is caught.

There is a tragic pathology involved. The diagnostician has to wonder over questions such as: How did UMNO, once a secular or at least non-religious party become a champion of religious politics?; How did the *relative* inter-ethnic harmony of the early decades end in the tensions in daily life that Malaysians now live with?; How has the acceptance of multiracialism as the basis of Malaysian life been overturned?; How did the cultured traditionalism of the Malays lose out to the harsh legalism of the Islamists?; Is it all the fault of the players or are external forces involved?

It would seem that it is knowledge of history that can lead the trapped fly out of the bottle; that can empty the sotong of ink.

Revisiting history unconditionally means an embracing of diverse interpretations of history, and that requires as many periodisations and rethinking of conditions as possible. New and substantive narratives become necessary.

Let me mention some unique historical conditions and periodisations to make my point and the reader can then taste their possibilities as he or she wishes:

- Just as the first 25 years of Malaysian history occurred with the Cold War as its backdrop, the second 25 years are shaped by the rise of China. How is this reflected in domestic politics?

- Malaysia was colonised in very unique and varied ways. The parts that made up the Straits Settlements came first. They were basically small bases functioning as part of the China trade to serve the European market. Then came other parts often ruled indirectly by the British –the federated states certainly more directly than the un-federated ones that switched from Thai control to British control to Japanese control, then back to British control and then to Malayan control. What indirect rule actually meant for states that were under it only for a few decades is an important point to consider. The East Malaysian states were even stranger, one being ruled by a timber company and the other by an English family. Sabah is also interesting in that it was bordered to the east by a part of the world that European colonialism reached only when it had run out of steam.

- All other parts of Southeast Asia (excepting Thailand to an extent) were also colonised and by other European powers. What did this cutting up of the region and the politicising of every square inch of territory do to the political consciousness of Southeast Asians?

- To what extent where the sultanates sovereign states and to what extent did some of them exist only as colonial creations? How does this affect how we should understand the Malayan Union and the level of colonisation that was visited on various Malay communities?

- How did the changing political conflicts and political concepts in Europe over the last few centuries affect the mode of colonisation and the nature of economic development in distant areas like Malaysia?

- To what extent do Southeast Asia's cultures reflect the influence in recent times of external powers, be this European, Chinese, Japanese or American? And to what extent is that a problem; to what extent a boon?

- What is nation-building in relation to state building in this part of the world?

- How have traditional understandings of power, ownership, political representation, communalism and statehood interacted with western notions of the same; and how does that effect how politics and power are understood and practised today?

- What are the long-term economic, cultural and political costs of the split between Malaysia and Singapore? How do these differ for the two?

There are many more such approaches to Malaysian history and self-understanding to consider, but I think you get the point. The over-politicisation of the Malaysian mind is a process of provincialisation. It keeps the katak under the tempurung—the frog under the coconut shell.

22

Waves from US Probe into 1MDB May Turn into Tsunami*

The civil lawsuits filed by the US Justice Department on 20 July 2016 to seize assets worth over US$1 billion stolen from Malaysia's state fund, 1MDB, are sending tight ripples across the globe.

Not only are these the largest set of cases brought to court under the Department's Kleptocracy Asset Recovery Initiative, the 1MDB fund started in 2009 ostensibly for national development purposes by Malaysian Prime Minister Najib Razak soon after he came to power, is being investigated in at least six other jurisdictions, including Singapore, Switzerland, Hong Kong and of course, Malaysia.

The alleged offenders involve 'an international conspiracy to launder money misappropriated from 1MDB', mentioned by US Justice Department include the Prime Minister's stepson Riza Aziz, the founder of Red Granite Pictures, whose film production 'The Wolf of Wall Street' was nominated for an Oscar, Malaysian financier Low Taek Jho and two government officials from Abu Dhabi, Khadem Abdulla Al-Qubaisi and Mohammed Ahmed Badawy Al-Husseiny.

In Malaysia, while the repercussions of alleged wrongdoings involving 1MDB have seen top politicians who had openly voiced criticism against the Prime Minister's handling of the fund sacked and other heavy-handed actions taken against whistle-blowers, all the legal avenues within the country for bringing perpetrators to court have proved ineffective.

---

* *The Straits Times*, Singapore, 22 July 2016.

Internationally, threats of legal action by Malaysian authorities against the Wall Street Journal, which had along with the London-based Sarawak Report website been publishing reports on the highly dubious behaviour of key persons in 1MDB's international network, had over many months been repeated but never carried out.

In Singapore, investigations into 1MDB have been noted by state prosecutors as 'the most complex and largest money laundering case ever to have taken place in Singapore'. The Monetary Authority of Singapore has withdrawn the license of the Swiss bank, BSI SA, to operate locally and senior BSI officials are being investigated. Two have been charged.

The details now provided in the cases filed by the US Justice Department are astonishingly thorough. These particulars delivered so publicly cannot but stimulate and hasten the execution of further legal actions in other countries, each building its case with help from revelations made by the others.

In Switzerland, the attorney general's office began investigations against two former Malaysian officials in August 2015 and have since indicted at least two further suspects. The Swiss allege that 1MDB had violated their embezzlement laws when money stemming from a fraudulent bond agreement it made with UAE officials was routed through Swiss banks. Switzerland has also asked Luxembourg and Singapore for assistance.

Luxembourg has also responded and is investigating whether hundreds of millions of dollars sent to one of its banks did in fact originate from 1MDB.

Hong Kong's anti-corruption agency as a rule does not provide details on cases under investigations but bank accounts there of unnamed individuals related to 1MDB were reportedly frozen in May this year.

In April this year, United Arab Emirates authorities froze the personal assets of two former officials of the US$80 billion Abu Dhabi investment fund called International Petroleum Investment Company (IPIC). These are those now named in the US lawsuits; Khadem Al Qubaisi, an Emirati who was managing director the Abu Dhabi and Mohammed Badawy Al Husseiny, an American who was also chief executive of another state investor called Aabar Investments PJS, which is part of IPIC.

In Malaysia, Prime Minister Najib was investigated after it became known that US$681 million had been transferred to a personal bank account apparently started for that purpose. This led to the investigating attorney-general Abdul Gani Patail being replaced. The new attorney general, Mohamed Apandi Ali, soon found the Prime Minister innocent of any crime.

The US lawsuits do state that US$681 million was transferred to the bank account of 'Malaysian Official 1', who was 'a high-ranking official in the Malaysian government who also held a position of authority with 1MDB'. The implication could not have been more direct, short of his name being mentioned.

In Malaysia, the 1MDB saga has had deep repercussions on the political scene and had led to strategies and counter-strategies between those opposed to the prime minister and those calling for a thorough and independent investigation into the goings-on of the ill-fated investment fund. It led former Malaysian Prime Minister Mahathir Mohamad to tour the country collecting signatures calling for the removal of his erstwhile protégé, Najib Razak. When this failed, Mahathir is taking the initiative to form a new political party to work with his former political enemies in the opposition parties to topple the Najib administration.

The ripples emanating from 1MDB across the world look poised to turn into waves, even a tsunami.

23

Seeking a New Formula to Unite Malaysia's Diversity*

The issue of Bangsa Johor, Johor nationality, made national news again on Wednesday, when former Prime Minister Mahathir Mohamad was asked about it at a forum on relations between the federal government and state governments.

Asked about Johor's separation from Malaysia, a national concern fanned by provocative comments made by Johor's Crown Prince, Tunku Ismail Sultan Ibrahim, Tun Dr Mahathir replied that such a separation would encourage 'unhealthy' feelings of superiority and harm the unity of the federation.

The issue of 'Bangsa Johor' is hugely interesting on several levels. It acts as a reminder that despite the centralised nature of Malaysian governance, the country was sewn together in the 1940s, 1950s and 1960s as a federation. This was clearly reflected in the country's 1957 Constitution.

This solution, worked out for a smooth decolonisation process, sought to acknowledge diversity while uniting a miscellany of state formations, identities and loyalties. Over the last half-century, however, much has happened to undermine this compromise.

The role of race champion that the Malay-based UMNO developed for itself quickly skewed the national inter-ethnic compromise and its consequent federal system to such an extent that being Malay became more important to most of its followers than becoming Malaysian.

---

* *The Straits Times*, Singapore, 26 August 2016.

It also led to the power-sharing system that united the nation's diverse groups from the very beginning being overwhelmed by the huge dominance of this ethnocentric party.

Not only had this train of events for decades been encouraging 'unhealthy feelings of superiority' among some Malaysians against others, but it also damaged the ability of the federation to argue for diversity as a strength. Instead, diversity became the country's major problem. And this diversity is as much intra-Malay as it is inter-ethnic or inter-regional.

The Johor case is symptomatic of this process having gone too far and occurs alongside other recent expressions of Malay opposition to UMNO power and to its self-proclaimed mandate to champion Malayness and Malaysianness.

These new expressions include Dr Mahathir's newly formed party, Parti Pribumi Bersatu Malaysia (Bersatu), not to mention Parti Amanah Negara recently established by dissidents from the Islamist party PAS or Anwar Ibrahim's Parti Keadilan Rakyat formed in the late 1990s.

One can argue that the call for federal devolution, if not separation, by Johor's Crown Prince and others, including many in the eastern state of Sabah, is in fact evidence of the failure of Dr Mahathir's own Bangsa Malaysia (Malaysian Nation), a popular concept that he championed in the 1990s alongside his vision of a mature Malaysia realised by 2020.

When Malaysia's impressive economic growth stalled during the 1997–98 financial crisis and the top leadership of UMNO split right down the middle, not only was the path towards Vision 2020 knocked off its trajectory, the idea that Malaysia would nurture a citizenry whose obsession with ethnic identity would be substantially lessened by its phenomenal economic success was also forgotten by UMNO.

Instead, that idea was adopted by those who rose up against Dr Mahathir and by younger Malaysians who were just coming of age following the sacking and jailing of his erstwhile deputy, Anwar, in the form of the goals of the Reformasi Movement.

This adoption inspired a shift in support away from the Barisan Nasional towards the opposition, but before that could gain momentum, UMNO under Tun Abdullah Badawi managed to convince voters to give the party one more shot at realising Vision 2020 and Bangsa Malaysia despite the financial crisis.

Tun Abdullah failed, as was shown by the ruling coalition's poor showing in the 2008 general election and pushed from within the party, he threw in the towel the following year.

His successor, Datuk Seri Najib Razak, immediately tried to regain the initiative through his slogan of One Malaysia. This appeared to lack sincerity and failed to gain traction among voters and when this became clear to him in the 2013 elections, he quickly abandoned that agenda.

Since then, racial and religious tensions have increased, while scandals with international repercussions have distracted and continue to distract the Najib government from proposing any new vision that can convincingly promise economic growth and social harmony.

Without such a promise coming from the federation's government, the constituent states are naturally anxious. This goes beyond inter-ethnic tensions or religious controversies. It is about the citizenry's need for a promising future.

Malaysia's dilemma thus remains the same – finding the right formula to unite the country without suppressing its diversity and doing it while achieving real and concrete economic growth.

None but the pathological optimist believes today that Malaysia will reach the economic goals of Vision 2020. The technical requirements and structural support are simply not sufficient.

Fortunately, the search for the right balance between centralised power and regional autonomy, between unity and diversity, follows a different set of dynamics.

The issue is political, and to the extent policy can change mindsets, much can yet be achieved quickly.

24

Time for Anwar to Accept Mahathir's Olive Branch*

Malaysia's former prime minister, Tun Dr Mahathir Mohamad, surprised his countrymen by turning up at the Kuala Lumpur High Court on Monday to shake the hand of his former deputy and protégé and (perhaps former) political foe, Anwar Ibrahim.

This is a highly significant event and their short meeting sent a strong impulse through the Malaysian political landscape. Since Dr Mahathir launched a campaign to unseat Prime Minister Najib Razak many months ago, including a national tour that succeeded in collecting beyond its target of a million signatures calling for the removal of the Prime Minister, it had been unclear how far his movement would take him. Or how far he would actually go in getting what he wants.

Strange twists in Malaysian politics now see the two figures who were once the two most powerful men in the country becoming fellow travellers with the common ambition of toppling the Prime Minister. The deep animosity between the two camps had loomed as the biggest hurdle to their forces mounting a concerted campaign against the federal government, and threatened to divide the opposition into those who would embrace Dr Mahathir into their camp, and those who refused.

It was an understandable divide, given that while Anwar's supporters wished to topple UMNO and not only Mr Najib, Dr Mahathir's supporters were only out to get rid of the Prime Minister.

---

* *The Straits Times*, Singapore, 8 September 2016.

85

The opposition parties, though having trouble working with each other, are largely faithful to Anwar and his agenda of national political reformation. No doubt, the grief that the former deputy prime minister and his family had had to suffer since his sacking on 2 September 1998 and eventual imprisonment accounts a lot for the sense of loyalty his supporters continue to feel for him.

His Reformasi Movement has after all been the inspiration for the generation of Malaysians from all ethnic backgrounds that now forms the backbone of the opposition.

In his dramatic move, Dr Mahathir appeared on neutral ground and over an issue that he and Anwar could agree upon, namely opposition to the National Security Committee (NSC) Act that they both claim gives unlimited powers to the Prime Minister.

Anwar was at the High Court on Monday to file an application to challenge the NSC Act and for once he was not there as the accused. It provided the best occasion for Dr Mahathir to be seen by the mass media and by Malaysians as the initiator of a conciliation, albeit a political one.

The public spectacle – and it was of course vital that it should be a public spectacle – of these two once-powerful figures shaking hands almost 18 years to the day since the younger man was sacked by the older man raised eyebrows, caused jaws to drop and sent pundits running to their keyboards to work out what all this will mean.

It is too soon after the breakthrough stretching of hands across the chasm to be sure of its aftermath. But given that Dr Mahathir had on 9 August started his own party, Parti Pribumi Bersatu Malaysia (Bersatu), saving UMNO by getting rid of Mr Najib may no longer be his goal. For Dr Mahathir, since UMNO and its network of power will not act against Mr Najib, his fight now has to be with UMNO as well.

In that sense, the two men's aims now overlap much more. Bersatu's potential – and that is why it was formed as a pointedly Malay-based part – lies in it being a reflection of UMNO itself. It has a clear strategic goal, which is to attract those Malays who are disenchanted with UMNO but who find it hard to accept any system that does not openly guarantee Malay rights.

If Bersatu seems able to deliver on that front, it is difficult, if not foolhardy, of Anwar and his supporters to reject Dr Mahathir's olive branch.

Dr Mahathir's decision to reach out to Anwar so publicly therefore makes it much easier for his erstwhile protégé to consider collaborating with the man who had caused him and his family so much suffering. Even for those who are deeply distrustful of Dr Mahathir, it is hard to deny that it was a commendable move by him to heal the rift, even if by just a little. His reasons, no doubt, are tactical, but if he stays steadfast in his claim that the country requires it, the resistance among opposition figures to work with him will definitely diminish.

25

Najib, Mahathir and the Timing of Malaysia's Polls*

According to its Constitution, Malaysia has to hold its next general election by 24 August 2018. At the time of writing, that is still almost two years away. And yet, rumours of early elections persist, both at the state and federal levels.

This needs some explaining, given how Prime Minister Najib Razak waited until almost the last minute to go to the polls back in 2013.

The exercise to delineate constituency boundaries now being concluded heightens speculation that early polls are coming. Having lost its two-thirds majority since 2008, the ruling Barisan Nasional (BN) has not been able to increase the number of parliamentary constituencies; it is now able only to realign the existing ones or rename them. And that, it is doing.

That in itself is a substantive exercise of power especially with the independence of the Election Commission that is in charge of the delineation being in serious doubt.

The major argument for those predicting that elections will be held by mid-2017 is that the opposition is in a confused state, if not in disarray. And so, before they can get their act together, the chances of Datuk Seri Najib holding his ground and maintaining at least the same voter support that he had in 2013 are good.

---

* *The Straits Times*, Singapore, 26 September 2016.

By hook or by crook, his administration has survived the many aspects of the 1Malaysia Development Berhad (1MDB) scandal, at least for now. By sacking key dissidents from UMNO, especially his former deputy Tan Sri Muhyiddin Yassin, he has consolidated his hold on the leadership of the party.

Victory in the Sarawak state election held in May and in two recent by-elections in June, one in Perak state which it marginally controls and the other in opposition-controlled Selangor state, also brought some comfort for the BN coalition and showed that the Malay ground remains encouragingly loyal. Also, the anti-BN votes in the by-elections were split down the middle between Parti Islam SeMalaysia (PAS) and its recent splinter party, Parti Amanah Negara.

Having this indication that the Malay opposition to UMNO is badly split and convinced that the PAS leadership is now more willing than ever to negotiate with it, BN has all the more reason to dissolve Parliament earlier rather than later.

While the founding of Parti Pribumi Bersatu Malaysia (PPBM) in August by Mr Muhyiddin and former Prime Minister Mahathir Mohamad to oppose UMNO may look like further fragmentation in Malay politics, the danger that PPBM poses to the ruling party is more real than in the case of Amanah.

PPBM has the clear tactical goal of enticing UMNO's middle rank to defect and the numbers who jump ship do not have to be big for sufficient parliamentary seats to go to the opposition. There have indeed been some defections at the grassroots level and it therefore makes good sense for BN not to take chances and instead plan for early elections to pre-empt any momentum that PPBM might be expected to gain.

UMNO and its allies cannot count on the opposition staying disunited and confused in the coming months.

But how is the opposition to unite, and quickly? The initiative seems to be with PPBM at the moment. The other opposition parties find themselves paralysed by internal disagreements –many over how they are to relate to Tun Dr Mahathir and PPBM. Furthermore, the fact that they have held power at state level for the last two terms (and more in the case of PAS in Kelantan state) makes them liable to strong criticisms over governance issues, especially as an election campaign approaches. Their moral high ground is definitely not as unassailable as it was one election ago.

Into that leadership vacuum step Dr Mahathir and PPBM.

Dr Mahathir shaking hands with Anwar Ibrahim in public and the two former allies and former foes signing a joint statement against the National Security Committee Act stunned many on all sides of the political divide. PPBM has also put forth the idea that the country's prime minister should not be allowed to stay beyond two terms. It also proposed that as a tactical move, a common election logo be adopted for all the opposition parties so that the choice for voters would become a simple one between BN and whatever the opposition group calls itself. Dr Mahathir's son, Datuk Seri Mukhriz Mahathir, has suggested 'Barisan Rakyat', which he claims is a name netizens prefer.

At present, the Democratic Action Party (DAP), Parti Keadilan Rakyat (PKR) and Amanah group themselves under Pakatan Harapan (PH). If the electoral pact were expanded to include PPBM – and more unlikely PAS, a new name may be needed. So, it could be BN versus BR, or BN versus PH.

Whichever strategy they choose and whatever forms of coalition building they may come up with, the opposition parties will have to avoid three-cornered fights if they are to convince fence-sitters to buy into their ambition of toppling BN and UMNO.

The major argument for those predicting that elections will be held by mid-2017 is that the opposition is in a confused state, if not in disarray. And so, before they can get their act together, the chances of Datuk Seri Najib holding his ground and maintaining at least the same voter support that he had in 2013 are good.

Supposing that Mr Najib is convinced that he will be returned to power, the next target for BN's electoral strategy – and that is always on as broad and deep a front as one can imagine – will be to regain the rich state of Selangor. Already, pundits are detecting in dismay that all else being equal, the delineation exercise will in itself push seven seats into BN's hands.

The DAP's hold on Penang is also not as strong as it was after 2008 and gaining any ground at all in that rebel state will be a breakthrough for the BN.

The national economy is not doing well either, and before it gets worse, it would be strategic of Mr Najib to go to the polls. The Budget that will be announced next month will provide clear signs as to whether elections will be called in the first half of next year or if Mr Najib will once again wait as long as he can.

Pressure from within and from outside the country is building up and the longer he waits, the less the options open to him become.

26

Excessive Governance is Not Good Governance[*]

The word 'Governance' has the same roots as 'Government'. However, the recent popularity of the use of 'governance' comes from the growing notion of looking at political control as a technical matter and of an increasing tendency to think of the government – and the governing – of a country as the management – and the managing – of a country.

We should also be aware that governance seems more at home in the context of corporations, and in line with that, the word assumes the existence of the entity to be unproblematic – be it a state or a corporation.

For countries and states that are relatively new and that are still being 'built', the increasing usage of 'governance' may be in response to the initial and over time, excessive focus on the notion of nation-building rather than on state building.

Governance as a notion necessarily highlights rules and regulations, technocratic mechanisms and corrective procedures. Except where security is a concern, it is of great advantage that information is free and reliable since policies have to be based on them – as are punishments.

So what constitutes Good Governance on the part of a national government?

---

[*] *The Edge*, Malaysia, 2 October 2016.

I would deconstruct the term into the following related processes:

1. State building (developing and maintaining the apparatus of the state);

2. Nation building (managing inter-ethnic ties; developing a sense of national belonging; handling extra-national relations);

3. National-economy building (integrating economic activities within the country; managing budget income and expenditure; investing for growth and economic stability);

4. Improving the socio-economic situation of the citizenry and maintaining a promise of a stable and better future;

5. Managing the relationship between state and citizenry (Rakyat), such that security and justice; freedom from fear; and protection from arbitrary power are maximised.

Each of these involves complicated and often strongly inter-linked itineraries. The focus differs from country to country and from regime to regime, and necessarily shifts over time as well.

The important point being made here is that the historical context of any given case must be considered in deciding what good governance is and is not.

Where building a state is concerned, the focus is mainly on technocratic capability and legal reliability. Building a nation, which is the more commonly adopted notion, deals more with the emotive aspects of social harmony and with matters of identity. Here, the areas for contention and contestation are many and are most open to politicisation.

Building a national economy today must involve the global economy. No man is an island and no economy can grow on its own. Modern China is a case in point. Despite its size, its economic development really began only with the opening up of its workforce to the international community; and it was the need to facilitate international trade that much of its present institutions and its legal system have come into being. In that important sense, China's state building and nation building have since 1980 been tied to the building of its national economy through international trade.

The income gap and the high level of corruption that ensued have now come to threaten China's continued growth, and so, reforms to achieve a higher level of governance have become necessary. These reforms seek to curb corruption and lessen the income gap while trying to broaden the basis for the country's economic development.

The size of the income gap measures in an effective way the socio-economic situation of the citizenry at large. Keeping the population at large fed is one thing, but just as important is the need to provide the present and next generation with hope for a good future.

Whether or not governance through all these simultaneous processes is good has to be judged by its historical situation. The concrete context in which a society finds itself in terms of social cohesion, economic dynamism and state capacity decides what needs doing, and what needs doing in that context would decide what policies are considered good.

Having said that, it should be noted that contexts are never static and good policies would therefore not merely be reactive but also normative and forward-looking. Furthermore, differences in historical context tend also to be often overplayed for political reasons. At the technical level, good governance is not rocket science and governments can in fact learn much from each other.

In conclusion, let me say that a discussion on good governance often errs in focusing too much on government action and not enough on the capacity of individuals and the ability of society to arrive at solutions that are for the common good. The state is not the only actor in society.

To push the point further, relying too much on the state and the government would lead to a preference for micromanagement. Now, micromanaging the behaviour of individuals and groups may be necessary for short periods under threatening conditions.

As a model for state or nation-building, it is bad governance indeed.

27

Why Malaysia's Opposition Will Take to the Streets Again[*]

Mass demonstrations are a strategic forcing of an issue to a head. This is definitely so in the case of Malaysia's Bersih 5 rally planned for 19 November. As its name reveals, this is the fifth street protest in a series.

Organised by a huge assemblage of civil society bodies, the first Bersih (Malay for 'clean') street march held on 10 November 2007, directly and simply called for clean and fair elections. That day, at least 30,000 yellow-shirted demonstrators turned up, with some having to endure chemical-laced water cannons for their troubles.

That demonstration turned a page in Malaysian politics and in the evolution of the country's civil society activism. It precipitated a political avalanche that almost swept the long-ruling Barisan Nasional (BN) coalition out of power in federal elections held the following year. The impetus continued, but again in the 2013 elections, the BN managed to cling on to power.

Bersih 5 goes beyond calling for clean elections and is instead a public show of outrage over how badly democracy has deteriorated in Malaysia. But unlike 2007, the diversity of forces arrayed behind it this time reflects the difficulties critics of the BN have faced in trying to dislodge a government they consider to have lost its moral mandate to rule.

---

[*] *The Straits Times*, Singapore, 10 November 2016.

Prime Minister Najib Razak's government, as a consequence of its weak position, has in the last few years applied a string of legal, paralegal, institutional and political means to silence powerful opponents. These have been surprisingly effective.

When he took power in 2009 in a party coup, Datuk Seri Najib's initial profile as leader was to reconcile traditional Malay-first aficionados with those gathered around former deputy prime minister Anwar Ibrahim who was preaching good governance as the cure-all for the country's many political ailments. Not only did Mr Najib fail to live up to this promise, his time in power has seen a worrying approval – and instigation – of dangerous expressions of racism and religious extremism.

In the general election of May 2013, Mr Najib had – albeit half-heartedly – focused his attention on winning back the Chinese electorate. After his narrow victory in those polls – no thanks to that electorate – he had asked angrily: 'Apa lagi Cina mahu?' (What more do the Chinese want?) His disappointment was great. The fault, as events since that night have shown, lay in his apparent failure to grasp why more than half the nation voted against the BN.

I would argue that there were two key reasons: the rise of Anwar's Pakatan Rakyat (PR) and the rejuvenation of civil society activism in Malaysia, and that these were more urban phenomena than race-based ones.

The critical need for the ruling BN to continue painting Bersih as a Chinese-based movement trying to topple a Malay rights government was most clearly seen in the fourth demonstration, held by the group on 29 August last year. That took place soon after the PR had fallen apart due to Parti Islam SeMalaysia (PAS) submitting a parliamentary Bill to legitimise hudud punishments in Kelantan state, with apparent BN backing.

Indeed, religious controversies in Malaysia have been plentiful, involving fantastic ones like the ban on non-Muslims using certain Muslim 'holy words' to grave ones like the rights of children of converts to Islam whose other parent is a non-Muslim. These are strongly entangled with inter-ethnic contentions, no doubt, with one feeding on the other.

The confusion in the wake of PR's demise saw a lessened presence of Malay faces at the demonstration, which provided an opportunity for Malay-rights extremists to counter-demonstrate and to reiterate that Bersih – and the Bersih movement in general – was a Chinese conspiracy. Former Prime Minister Mahathir Mohamad turning up in support of that Bersih rally did nothing to weaken that allegation.

A Malay-dignity movement quickly sprang up to buttress the conspiracy claim against the Bersih movement and its red-shirted followers marched the following month to Chinese enclaves in Kuala Lumpur. Strangely, the hesitant authorities acted to rein them in only after Beijing's ambassador to Malaysia, Mr Huang Huikang, acting against diplomatic propriety, spoke out against the threat while visiting the city's Chinatown.

The dissolution of PR quickly led to progressive leaders in PAS breaking away to form Parti Amanah Negara and remaining loyal to the governance ideals of the old coalition. This party helped form the replacement coalition, Pakatan Harapan (Fellowship of Hope).

UMNO, the mainstay of BN, had suffered its own split following Anwar's sacking in 1998 and it was in fact that splinter party, Parti Keadilan Rakyat, that allowed for PR to form in 2008.

The political equation got more complex when Tun Dr Mahathir together with his son Mukhriz and recently sacked Deputy Prime Minister Muhyiddin Yassin formed a new Malay-based party, Parti Pribumi Bersatu Malaysia (PPBM, Malaysian United Indigenous Party). Unlike the other new Malay-led parties, which chose to use terms like 'justice', 'trust' and 'hope' in their names and reiterate words such as 'competence', 'accountability' and 'transparency', PPBM appears revisionist in appealing to 'indigeneity' in its name.

Tactically, this makes perfect sense. PPBM is an emotional appeal to UMNO members who have not yet acted on their disenchantment with Mr Najib and hopes to provide the tipping point that will bring the government down.

The strong representation of former UMNO members in its supreme council is a clear indication of the party's wherewithal. In a move calculated to appease doubting Anwaristas, Dr Mahathir recently arranged a short meeting with Anwar in public and in front of cameras during which the two men shook hands amid smiles. The wives of the two men have also met again, for the first time in 18 years.

But the battle between parties and coalitions is just one side of the coin. The deeper dynamic in Malaysian society today is socio-economic and ethical in nature and expresses itself in social media squabbles, in increased emigration and in angrier civil societal activism. Given how Mr Najib has managed to survive the 1Malaysia Development Berhad (1MDB) scandal and in the process to further undermine the integrity of key national institutions, the options for civil society and regime critics to act effectively are few.

As long as the country's 'state of transition' drags on and on, no proper discussion about nation-building going one way or the other can take place, and things are bound to get worse if they are not forced to get better. It is in that context that the Bersih 5 rally is best seen. If the aces are all in Mr Najib's hand, then a joker is needed.

28

Merdeka is About the Individual, Too*

Malaya gained independence on 31 August 1957 and Malaysia on September 16, 1963. Those historic dates mark the end of British colonial control over the Malay Peninsula and northern Borneo.

More significantly, they mark the beginning of painful but hopeful times for the citizens and the leaders of the new country. They point forward, not backwards to the past.

In general academic parlance, a twin process of state building and nation building kicked in at those points. (I have discussed these matters before in this column, so I will skip the details here.)

However, there are other aspects of independence that are often considered – not only in Malaysia but in most new nations to be of low priority, whose development is therefore actually ignored or even consciously hampered.

The question that needs asking then is: 'Why independence?'

The answer to that very important question is twofold. Firstly, the issue simply regards the question of self-determination. Freedom from external control and abuse was the immediate objective.

But what about the longer term?

Beyond the interest of state and nation lie the interests of the individual – the citizen, if you like. In the rush to build nation and

---

*   *The Edge*, Malaysia, 5–11 December 2016.

state, what was a major point in gaining Merdeka – namely the development of the individual Malaysian citizen as an independent and intelligent modern person capable of handling modern challenges – has been neglected.

If we reduce state building to a matter of security, and nation building to one on identity, and the both of them synchronised as a matter of economic growth, we see how the development of the integrity of the individual Malaysian is overshadowed, notwithstanding the rhetoric.

It can be argued that the long-term goal of Merdeka is the empowerment of the individual – not of the state, not of the nation, not of the economy. Those are processes that pave the way. They are the means. The end is the creation of citizens imbued with a strong sense of integrity. That was what Bangsa Malaysia was aiming at.

And that is why rights such as the freedom of assembly, the freedom of association and the freedom of speech are so vital. They allow for citizens to experience and nurture their sense of agency. But sadly, that is also why these rights tend to be so excessively curbed within systems professing narrow views on economic growth, political stability and social unity.

But in diminishing these rights, the essential role that they play in developing the self-confidence, sense of integrity and the agency of the individual is diminished, and an essential goal of Merdeka is denied.

In short, the fewer chances you have of expressing your thoughts to others, the less are you able to develop them over time and the less are you able to feel that you are the equal of others who enjoy those rights more than you are able to do so. So when Malaysians call for change today, they do not only mean that they want the political system to evolve or incumbent leaders to retire. They are demanding a social, legal and cultural milieu that allows them to make full use of Merdeka.

The Merdeka process started as political liberation while its long-term aim is to empower the individual citizen while avoiding the very real danger of domestic suppression by the new political elite.

Do we then end up with a zero-sum game of the political elite versus the rakyat?

The political elite, like the rakyat, is heterogenous, and life is about individuals facing off other individuals and groups facing off other groups.

The state, in essence, is the mediator between individuals and groups. In fact, one of its main duties is to work out consistent rules and policies for minimising conflict, establish the space for individual development to co-exist with inter-individual struggle and for groups to interact peacefully with groups.

That is why you have the rule of law. That is why you have due process in making laws, monitoring laws, amending laws and punishing offences. For all this to have legitimacy, you require freedom of expression, freedom of association and free speech.

That is the end to which Merdeka is the means. Not to create the state as such, nor to free the individual as such but to attain and maintain a situation that nurtures a healthy symbiosis between the two.

29

A Battle Between Malay leaders Over Malaysia's Future[*]

The year 2016 is about over.

It was a year of surprises globally, what with terrorist attacks in Europe, the refugee flows into Europe from the Middle East, Brexit, the election of Donald Trump as the next US president and so on.

For Malaysia, it was allegations and investigations, and sackings and jailings surrounding the 1Malaysia Development Bhd (1MDB) investment fund run by Prime Minister Datuk Seri Najib Razak that were given the most column inches and the most browser space in the traditional and social media.

Tied to this was the low-key celebration of the seventieth anniversary of the founding of the dominant party, the United Malays National Organisation (UMNO). This should not surprise observers since the party has in fact been plagued by serious internal strife and its president has been under tremendous pressure to explain the goings-on involving 1MDB. Sadly, the 1Malaysia slogan that he so hopefully adopted after taking power in 2009 is now cause for ridicule and criticism.

A totally new political scenario has been building up over the last two years, and despite Najib's and UMNO's amazing ability to survive challenges that in most other countries would have seen a change of government many times over, there is likely little chance that the ruling coalition can increase its voter support.

---

[*] *The Edge*, Malaysia, 26 December–1 January 2016.

UMNO's challenges are serious indeed, and they have been coming fast and furious. We saw the removal, among others, of its deputy president Tan Sri Muhyiddin Yassin as deputy prime minister in June 2015 and his sacking from the party in July 2016. Since then, Muhyiddin has joined former prime minister Tun Dr Mahathir Mohamad who had resigned from the party in February 2016 after his son Datuk Seri Mukhriz Mahathir was dumped as Menteri Besar of Kedah. Mukhriz was later sacked from the party along with Muhyiddin.

In September, these three, together with other former UMNO members, formed a new Malay-based party, Parti Pribumi Bersatu Malaysia (PPBM). And on Dec 13, PPBM most significantly signed an electoral agreement with the opposition coalition, Pakatan Harapan.

Over in Sabah, Shafie Apdal, the UMNO vice-president who was removed from the Rural and Regional Development portfolio when Muhyiddin lost his Cabinet position in July 2015, formed an opposition party of his own, the Sabah Heritage Party (Warisan).

And lest we forget, Mahathir and Datuk Seri Anwar Ibrahim have shaken hands publicly in what should be seen as the maximal level of conciliation one can expect for now between the two leaders, who now find themselves fronting the oppositional forces arrayed against Najib.

And with that, the political stage is more or less set for 2017.

What Malaysia watchers will be looking out for in the coming months will be an announcement by the prime minister on the dissolution of Parliament and subsequently the date for the fourteenth general election. This will immediately set in motion an avalanche of activity among the opposition parties. Negotiations for seats and constituencies should have all been concluded by then.

Where the Barisan Nasional parties are concerned, their preparations for the election campaign tend to start much earlier and on the sly, although customarily, news of this leak out as vendors are tasked with orders to provide them with campaign paraphernalia.

While Malaysian politics may have always been about inter-ethnic divides, the new stage on which the fourteenth general election will be performed will manifest the political crossroads at which the Malay community – and therefore Malaysia in general – finds itself today.

With the size of the non-Malay population sharply diminishing over the years, coupled with the urbanisation and the rise in educational levels of the very young Malay community as well as the disruptions to information control wrought by social media and the internet, the political arena is now one where the fiercest and most decisive battles are fought between Malay leaders and Malay groups.

The continued use of the Chinese and DAP bogeyman aside, the deep trenches are within the Malay community. This should not be unexpected and in many ways are the long-term results of the successes of the New Economic Policy. At the same time, and just as unexpected, many of the issues plaguing the Malay community are in essence about the worst negative consequences of the NEP and the debilitating culture of privilege, patronage and entitlement that it facilitated and that has come to infect the institutions of government.

In that very real sense, the coming election is a battle for Malaysia's future, a battle that will decide whether or not Malaysia will have a future reminiscent in some way of Vision 2020.

Leaving behind the old bogeymen and old defences in order to confront underlying realities is the difficult psychological and political dilemma that the Malay community, now clearly divided into two equal camps, needs to resolve – and quickly.

And after the election, working towards a conciliatory and viable solution that will enhance the national economy on the global stage will be the big challenge for Malay leaders on all sides.

30

The Primacy of Political Economy in Asia*

It is a complicated subject, this thing we call Economics. I do not always know what it means.

I remember once talking to Robert Kuok about it. His reply was (and I paraphrase from my vague memory of that conversation): 'Economics is simply about living, isn't it? As you live, you learn to live – that is economic knowledge'.

That is the gist of what I understood from what he said. I offer my apologies if I misunderstood his point. But what I understood then made sense to me. In fact, his description comes very close to the original meaning of the term. 'Economics' has Greek origins, coming from the word okionomia, which means 'household management'.

However, no household exists by itself, and so Economics cannot be about the management of a single household. It has to deal with the management of multiple households. The existence of multiple households means politics, of course. Therefore, when the subject of Economics emerged as a distinct modern field of study, it went under the title of 'political economy'. Such was the case when Scottish economists Adam Smith (1723–90) and David Hume (1711–76) and the French thinker Francois Quesnay (1694–1774) made their greatest contributions by using systematic and secular terms to explain the creation and maintenance of wealth by studying the complex interactions between political, social, economic and technological factors.

---

* Editorial, *Penang Monthly*, July 2017.

Since then, Economics as an academic discipline has branched out in many directions and there is really no definition of Economics today that anyone calling himself an economist agrees on. One can see why. If the focus is on the individual household, then we see how Smith's notion of 'the Invisible Hand' can argue how the collective effect of self-interest also serves the common good. For some, this approach ignores the state a little too much and disregards what we today see as a central tenet of political and economic studies – National Interests.

The preference for the individual in understanding economics was further undermined by Karl Marx (1818–83), who put forth powerful arguments that economic trends and dynamics are best understood as part and parcel of an unending class struggle within any societal form.

Today, when we talk about Political Economy, we silently assume that we are doing something unconventional, and following the interdisciplinary fad, are putting two distinct subjects together. And yet, in Asian societies and in newly formed nations, politics and economics are seldom unconnected matters. The fact that Asian governments almost always create government-linked corporations (GLCs) of various formats to compete against the multinational corporation (MNCs) of developed countries makes Political Economy the natural field of study of Asian life.

We seem to be struggling in the post-Cold War era on the one hand with a 'cosmopolitan' system (as the economist Friedrich List described Smith's obsession with the 'invisible hand') that now comes in the form of neoliberal economics and on the other with the idea that the state – politics – is paramount.

When Dr Goh Keng Swee (1918–2010), Singapore's economic tsar, proclaimed 'the primacy of economics' in constructing the modern city-state in the 1960s, he was not denying the primacy of politics. He in fact assumed the state to be the prime actor in his economic innovations. What he dreaded was that the state in its nation-building eagerness – politics – would deny the importance of economics – the management of households.

One could say that Mao Zedong did make that fatal error and it was Deng Xiaoping who succeeded in 1978 in establishing economics as the top priority of the state, communist or not. Economics today is of course about international trade and international supply chains.

In the case of Malaysia, Political Economy is indeed also the most valid social science. The problem is that the Malaysian state is more often than not taken to be the ruling party. And so, we observe the party economy more than the Malaysian economy being invested in. Worse yet, the state is very often considered to be the ruling party leadership, in which case what we observe is the management of a party-elite economy instead of a Malaysian economy or even a party economy.

The huge income gaps we now have in Malaysia and in Singapore come from the historical project of building a national economy –a state economy, where the management of households is done from the top down. Politics as the management of a collection of proactive households gets forgotten.

Mahathir at the Helm

31

One Thing is Certain—There Will Be More Amendments to the Constitution[*]

As with all agreements, consensus and contracts, a Constitution is a hunt for a balance – and a dynamic one at that, between the expressing on one hand of lofty national aspirations and ambitions, and on the other of compromises meant to be more binding than they usually turn out to be.

It is an act of self-definition and self-control, where rights and duties are laid out in broad generic terms. Thus, one can see it either as a search for common ideals, or as an arena of contestation where the fortunes of different interest groups shift over time. Which parts are carved in stone and which parts are of wet clay? That seems to be the unanswerable question.

Edmund Burke, the famous conservative and vivid scholar of the French Revolution wrote in 1790 in Reflections on the Revolution in France that 'A state without the means of some change is without the means of its conservation. Without such means it might even risque the loss of that part of the constitution which it wished the most religiously to preserve.'

The obsession that Malaysian political parties have about the two-thirds majority in parliament is a clear reflection that the country's Constitution is an arena of contestation rather than an expression of

---

[*] Editorial, *Penang Monthly*, August 2017.

common ideals. Having the means to amend the Constitution is what power seems to be about.

One can certainly argue that the contingencies of the 1950s – the fear of communism, the rush to gain independence on the part of the Malayan leaders and the need of the British to let its empire fall into a pattern that still left it with serious advantages, made the basic law of the country-to-be a balancing act – a superb act in legal formulation – that allowed most citizens to feel that they had not been excessively ignored.

As we know, the choice for Malaya of a federation model instead of a union model – a decision reached in the immediate post-war period rather than after the communists had been largely defeated in the mid-50s, was not so much a matter of political principle and academic wisdom than it was the expression of the British need to retain the status quo of having sultanates. After all, the nature of nation-building and the uncertainties of the times would have been better managed through the creation of a strong central government that could construct a vibrant economy, unite society and keep the peace – domestically and against outside forces. And a union model would seem the appropriate one for that.

The ethnic diversity of Malaya – soon to be amplified by integration with Sarawak, Sabah and Singapore (on and then off in the last case), remained the festering problem that would not leave the Constitution alone. While the federative delineation along sultanate lines reflected the very recent history of British administration over the peninsula, the centralised government under an UMNO-controlled ethnicity-based coalition grew out of the urgency of British withdrawal and the rush by Malayan leaders to fill the political vacuum that threatened.

Differences had to be put aside, if only for just a little while.

The Malaysian Constitution, assembled under such conditions, was an impressive attempt at turning a rickety sampan into a well-welded steamer that would equip a strong central government with the means to lead the country towards economic growth and political stability.

Amendments to Constitutions are not something unique. Far from it. In the Malaysian case, seen against the backdrop of the country's complex and contentious historical situation, these were bound to come. And they did come, quick and fast.

The Alliance and then the Barisan Nasional in its advocacy of consensus under Malay oversight developed as the arena in which changes, especially to the Malaysian Constitution (literally, the nature of Malaysia) could be worked out over time. Parliament, then, would be nothing more than a rubber stamp. The real contest, the real arguing would take place within the ruling coalition.

For this one-coalition system to work, the two-thirds majority rule needed for constitutional amendments became the real battlefront. The BN thus managed always, by hook or crook, to retain a two-thirds majority all the way until 2008.

That is why Malaysia is now at the crossroads. The overwhelming dominance of UMNO within BN was what caused the BN model itself to begin collapsing through its failure to express the diverse wishes of the population at large.

What is to come will be a renewed contest to construct a model that either reverts to the old consociational system, or to alternatives that allow the spirit of federalism to be properly expressed. Whichever the case, more amendments to the Constitution are to be expected.

32

The More Things Change, the More Things May Actually Change*

The elections are coming, and the array of political parties facing each other across the widening divide can be stupefying for any observer newly arrived on the Malaysian scene.

It would seem therefore that a quick look at the historical context in which some of Malaysia's major political parties came into being would provide some badly needed understanding of where the country's politics is heading.

Let us start with UMNO. The United Malays National Organisation started out in 1946 in reaction to Britain's fateful eagerness to rearrange its colonies into a manageable form following its diminished capacity to rule an empire following the Second World War.

The hasty and underhanded manner in which it implemented the Malayan Union that year, partially based on a faulty understanding of the basis of its authority in Malaya led to a revolt by the Malay community. Occurring as it did at a time when the rest of the Malay Archipelago was undergoing a surge of republican, leftist and anti-colonial violence, the British quickly had second thoughts and swung as hastily in the other direction. And so, the Federation of Malaya quickly came into being in early 1948.

The chaotic reality on the ground, however, soon forced the architects of the Federation to Malaya Agreement to search for a middle ground where ethnic relations and ideology were concerned.

---

* *The Edge*, Malaysia, 28 August 2017.

On the side of the Chinese community, the political situation over recent decades had left them with influential local branches of political parties that had been fighting the Japanese in Mainland China, while the Indian community had on the one hand been excited by India's independence in 1947 and on the other radicalised by Subhas Chandra Bose's Indian National Army during the war.

To cut a long story short, the Malayan Chinese Association (MCA) was formed in 1949 to organise and unite anti-communist elements from among the Straits Chinese and from the local Kuomintang under one umbrella; and the Malayan Indian Congress (MIC), inspired by Mahatma Gandhi's Indian National Congress, came into being just after the war. UMNO and MCA, with MIC joining in 1955, became the backbone of the consociational system we know as the Alliance, which won the election so convincingly that year that the British had little official reason left not to grant independence to its assortment of colonies on the peninsula.

UMNO however saw its more religious following break away in late 1951 to form Persatuan Islam Se-Malaya (PAS). Apparently, the religiously neutral attitude that allowed for all the necessary inter-ethnic and cross-ideological compromises was not to their liking.

The 1960s that followed were turbulent times of a different order, which saw disarray among leftist parties like the Labour Party and those that formed the Socialist Front. That period also saw Singapore's PAP joining the fray in 1963 and then leaving it in 1965, all the while fronting the 'Malaysian Malaysia' concept. Singapore's withdrawal from Malaysia necessitated the founding of the Democratic Action Party (DAP), while internal struggles in the MCA led to the formation of the tiny United Democratic Party in 1962 and then the much more successful Parti Gerakan Rakyat Malaysia in 1968.

The arrival of these new parties proved to be a strong challenge to the Alliance, and after the racial riots that followed the electoral defeats it suffered in 1969, inter-party confrontations were brought almost to a standstill through the formation of the Barisan Nasional. This roped in all parties that would agree to join from both East and West Malaysia, sometimes under duress. This included Gerakan. Even PAS became a member until it broke away in dismay in December 1977. The only prominent party that refused to be incorporated was the DAP.

In the state of Perak, the People's Progressive Party that was founded in 1953, joined the Alliance for a year but withdrew in 1955 over disagreements over the allotment of seats. Popularly supported by the Chinese population and led by Indian lawyers, it would have formed the state government in Perak with the help of other opposition parties were it not for the defection of two of its members. The party felt compelled to join the BN in 1973, only to lose all its seats in the elections the following year.

The only occasions when significant challenges to the BN could be mounted were when there were splits in UMNO. The first time was in 1990 when Tengku Razaleigh Hamzah took on then-Prime Minister Mahathir Mohamad through the formation a year earlier of Semangat '46, and its two coalitions – Gagasan Rakyat formed with the DAP and Parti Rakyat Malaysia (PRM); and Angkatan Perpaduan Ummah made up of PAS, Berjasa and Hamim as well as the newly formed Malaysian Indian Muslim Congress (KIMMA). The PRM was a party established already in 1955 whose democratic socialist roots were in the anti-colonial movements of the pre-war years. The dual coalitional challenge had an impact but failed nevertheless, as would the next anti-BN challenge two elections later, which was of course in the wake of Anwar Ibrahim's sacking as Deputy Prime Minister in 1998.

The repercussions of that momentous split in 1998 between Malaysia's two most powerful leaders opened floodgates that pulled along all in its path.

Since Anwar's sacking and imprisonment in 1998–99, three new parties have come into being. The Reformasi movement surrounding Anwar led to the formation of the multiracial Parti Keadilan Nasional in 1999, which in 2003 merged with PRM to form Parti Keadilan Rakyat (PKR). In the 1999 elections, Keadilan, PAS and DAP contested as Barisan Alternatif, which gave the BN a run for its money. The results of the 2004 elections, however, saw the BN making a strong comeback after Mahathir's retirement the year before.

In 2008, it was suddenly the opposition's turn. PKR, PAS and DAP won surprising successes at the state level and took power in five states. The Pakatan Rakyat coalition consequently formed by them continued putting pressure on the BN federal government to the extent of winning the popular vote in 2013.

Since then, further splits have taken place. First, Pakatan Rakyat fell apart in June 2015 following PAS insistence on pushing the hudud issue. Then PAS itself split when its group of progressives broke away after losing badly in party elections, to take over and transform the small Parti Pekerja-Perkerja Malaysia into Parti Islam Amanah Negara (Amanah) in September 2015.

The newest party on the Malaysian scene is the one founded in September 2016 by Mahathir together with sacked and disenchanted members of UMNO. It has since joined the DAP, PKR and Amanah to form the new coalition – Pakatan Harapan.

What quick lessons can we learn from this quick sketch of political parties? For starters, the difference between PKR and Bersatu is of great interest. When Anwar refused to exit the scene and chose to fight Mahathir in 1998, he and his followers understandably took a stance that was the polar opposite of what UMNO under Mahathir then stood for. They adopted slogans highlighting good governance, justice, transparency and accountability. When the time came for the retired Mahathir to challenge UMNO, he positioned it as close to it as possible ideologically. It was a 'same-same-but-different' strategy, in contrast to Keadilan's idealistically 'totally-something-else' approach.

What we now have then, is a recognisable and common showdown between two coalitions. But something is novel here, nevertheless. We have for the first time in West Malaysian history, five Malay-based or Malay-led parties contending for the Malay vote. On one side, we have UMNO and PAS, two race-based parties founded before independence and who have had a love-hate relationship with each other or as long as one can remember; and on the other, we have three parties – PKR, Amanah and Bersatu, all founded recently following splits form the first two parties.

The DAP today may appear to represent the large portion of the greatly reduced minority Chinese, but as always, it is the Malay majority that will determine much of what happens politically. That community's apparent splintering into groups may bode ill for agendas that rely on intra-ethnic loyalty and on singularity in political support, but it suggests a confidence in the community which is now not easily shaken by claims that the Malays as a race are under threat from their non-Malay compatriots. Of course, it also reflects a serious loss of faith in the old BN model's ability to achieve for the race and the country, a global stature Malays can be proud of.

This willingness among the Malays to split so drastically may actually make race-based politicking less effective in the future. To be sure, it may be in response to this Malay race-championing since the 2013 electoral scare suffered by BN and Prime Minister Najib Razak has turned so much into narrow Muslim faith-championing instead.

33

Did Merdeka Liberate or Create Malaya?*

Sixty years may have passed since Merdeka Day, but its historical significance remains something we continue to debate.

Did Malaya fight to free itself from an implacable Britain? Did the British offer independence to its colonies in South-East Asia to suit its own ends? Was there a Malaya that now threw off the shackles of Pax Britannia's global hegemony? Or was Malaya something novel, grown out of generations of colonial conveniences?

In short, the key question is: 'Was there a Malaya that on 31 August 1957, was liberated and granted independence? If there already was a Malaya, in what sense was there one? Or was it created that day? If it was created that day, what were the ingredients – physical and cultural – that went into the concoction?'

The Legal Malaya

The trouble taken to so carefully craft a national constitution under the oversight of an international commission would suggest that a new polity was in fact being judiciously brought into being and that nothing like it had existed before. Seen that way, the constitution was the outlining of a new entity we would now call the Federation of Malaya, an act of definition in fact that was geared towards immediate membership in the UN.

---

* Editorial, *Penang Monthly*, September 2017.

Already on 17 September 1957, the country became the eighty-first member of the United Nations. Needless to say, most of those members who came later and many of those who went before were in fact new countries, generated and necessitated by the fall of empires and of colonies throughout the twentieth century.

Gaining political existence in a form that would gain the country immediate membership to the UN was a basic deliberation in the crafting of the Malayan Constitution. What qualities a country should essentially possess for it to be a potential member were what the lawyers and politicians involved in crafting the document were trained to consider.

The UN has 193 members today, up from 80 before 31 August 1957, 60 years ago. How so many diverse societies in the world could over just a few decades after the demise of the imperial principle of human organisation take on the strict stock character of the nation-state, explains much of the global troubles that we live with today – not only in Malaysia but throughout the world. What the alternatives could have been and can be are still being worked out violently and painfully every day especially in the 25 years since the communist model a la Marx-Engels-Lenin-Stalin-Mao fell apart.

With Pax Americana weakening today a multipolar system seems impending but what that actually means for newly constructed nation states and their globally connected economies is hard to predict.

The Political Malaya

We should remember that the major criterion for the British Foreign Office struggling with the deterioration of Britain's post-war economy in deciding to 'grant independence to Malaya' or to 'create Malaya', was that a stable enough political solution was on offer as well.

Handing over power to a political structure that could not only defeat communists on the Malayan peninsula but also stay spiritually true to the letter of the constitutional compromise were what concerned the British greatly.

The Alliance consociationalism that evolved in the mid-1950s was therefore a brilliant innovation on the part of local politicians who understood the lay of the land and it provided a quick and hopeful alternative to the British whose Malayan Union model had failed so badly in the mid-1940s.

Malaya – and more so Malaysia – was therefore a bold compromise, a modern creation configured by assorted cultural and colonial contexts.

As global dynamics change, the defining of Malaysia – and the deciding of what Merdeka means – will therefore continue *ad infinitum*.

34

Interview with Nurul Izzah Anwar: Rebuilding a Nation Long Divided*

Nurul Izzah, Daughter of the Reformasi, and of the jailed opposition leader Anwar Ibrahim, was pulled into politics as a young girl. Now 36 years old, she has become a major figure in Malaysian politics. The future looks bright for her and many see her as a future prime minister. Sometimes called a giant killer for her electoral successes, she had had to suffer much over the last two decades.

She and her mother Wan Azizah Wan Ismail, chairman of Pakatan Harapan, visited Penang Institute on 29 July 2017 to attend its event, 'Symposium Pemikiran Anwar Ibrahim: Penampilan Demokrat Muslim'. *Penang Monthly* took the chance to chat with both of them.

* * *

Ooi Kee Beng: Thank you for taking the time to meet me. Should I call you Nurul or Izzah?

Nurul Izzah Anwar: Izzah. We are five girls and one boy, and all the girls have 'Nurul' in their name. Nurul just means 'Light of' in Arabic, so you need another name to go with it. [Izzah means Might or Power].

OKB: The last time we met was at a lunch following a talk in December last year at the Rajaratnam School of International Studies in Singapore. The Pakatan coalition at that time was not in good shape, I remember. Today as we meet, the picture looks very different. After July 14 this year, Pakatan Harapan looks promising after the parties

---

* *Penang Monthly*, September 2017.

managed to agree on the coalition's power structure. Do you feel it is more hopeful than Pakatan Rakyat was?

NIA: These are in different contexts and it would be flawed if we equate these developments to be one and the same. In 2008 the opposition obtained an agreement for one-to-one fights across the board and Pakatan Rakyat came into being only after the results proved impressive. And then there was agreement on a policy framework that bound everyone together. Pakatan Harapan (PH) came about after a split in PR. There was a trust deficit and a degree of cynicism had permeated the scene. Therefore there was greater urgency to galvanise ourselves especially since Anwar Ibrahim, the leader of the opposition, had been imprisoned. Every opposition per se would face problems of cohesion; we are not exempted from that. So I would say, Tun Dr Mahathir Mohamad and the other old warlords who had been ejected from UMNO eventually coming together in the party called Bersatu provided an opportunity for them to join our new coalition. So, it's a very different situation. You are looking at former victims of Mahathir coming together with the perpetrator…

OKB: It's a very strange situation.

NIA: Strange, but we are left with limited options. Therefore it goes back on the institutions that have to be quickened in pace to be further strengthened because they act as bulwarks against possible derailment of any reform agenda. You are dealing with players who are frenemies, ya. They are not traditional allies and so you have a different socialisation process. We have to prove we are different. In order for any coalition to work, there has to be some degree of trust built because we are not just about winning elections. We have to win hearts and minds and eventually rebuild a nation that has long been divided. I would argue the bulwark has to be civil society, different stakeholders and the reform agenda itself. Citizens and civil society shouldn't shy away; they shouldn't be quick to dismiss things; they should be reminded of their own role in all of this and [be encouraged] to participate even more than before, precisely because of the dynamics that have come about.

OKB: What I can sense after July 14 is a new buzz. People are seeing that maybe PH is getting their act together.

NIA: A sense of excitement is all well and good. But it is also a tragedy for a nation to be such a victim of the politics of 'Divide-and-Rule'. We are such a victim, otherwise why would Mahathir be a choice, even as chairman of PH? Things are so polarised and starkly so. People in the north of the peninsula are different, people in East Malaysia are different; and they have their own complacent normalisation. They feel quite comfortable with certain leaders to the extent that it really suppresses the emergence of new talents.

OKB: I remember 2008. It was the coming of a new generation. But two elections later, we have the oldest politician around [fronting the opposition]…

NIA: Maybe because you can't really take a shortcut; you can't short-circuit. But I am hopeful. For me, it is also the undoing of the enigma of Mahathir. He has to learn from it and to remedy things through his actions.

OKB: He has been seeing the things he thought he had nailed into place before he retired unravelling before his eyes, hasn't he? So he went against former prime minister Tun Abdullah Ahmad Badawi, he went against Datuk Seri Najib Razak…

NIA: Well, who knows? People can only guess as to the motives. But you can judge by their actions. It's still early days. What is crucial is the nurturing of the processes of decision-making. How else can we guide [developments]; how else can we guard against any derailment of the reform agenda? Of course people are excited, but if you look at any movement, be it the Arab Spring or the Iranian Revolution, never overestimate the importance of any particular personality.

OKB: Yes, of course. When we talk about movements, we are talking about people moving, a whole society moving. At the same time, you do have personalities who manage to capture the tenor of the times, the lay of the land at a precise moment. In that context, your meeting with Mahathir in London was watched with great interest here in Malaysia, I think. Would you be willing to say something about that?

NIA: We have to be guided by conscience; and we have to be guided by our sense of purpose and prioritise the nation's well being. I knew that people were expecting a clear-cut, cohesive coalition. We have had our issues; we can't afford only vague interactions between the coalition parties. Therefore, I felt we were at a stalemate, ya. I was going to be in London anyway, and [Mahathir] happened to be there. I felt that it was crucial to engage continuously and it does not mean that we are seeking his support or agreement. But it would showcase that there are many areas where we have consensus, on many things within the reform agenda. And I would like to carry that message forward. For me, regardless of what happened in the past – and I don't mean we should forget the past – it is still important for Mahathir to understand what had happened and one way to do that is through engagement – for him to understand the system and the flaws that he allowed as enablers for Najib's [misdeeds].

OKB: Was that what you met him to talk about?

NIA: First and foremost, you have to create a bond. You create a bond and then people understand what your concerns are. Rome wasn't built in a day.

OKB: You grew up at a time when Mahathir and Anwar were very close, right?

NIA: I was in government school and we met once a year for a meal. But of course, Mahathir was the prime minister of my generation, right? I am of Generation Mahathir, in a sense. Back then I felt very proud of our government but of course, there were many problems. And these were highlighted by my schoolmates in Assunta [Secondary School in Petaling Jaya] – how national heritage was being destroyed, the issue of Bakun Dam, corruption, cronyism. I think 1998 was very important because it was a wake-up call. I grew up alongside activists – from Suaram, from Abim. It really helped forge a deep realisation and commitment on my part to the understanding that Malaysia needed reforming. In Islam, constant renewal is taught to be a normal thing, through which you strengthen your resolve and improve outcome.

OKB: It was in London that Mahathir said he didn't mind your father becoming the prime minister, right?

NIA: He did, in an interview with The Guardian.

OKB: Was that connected to your meeting with him?

NIA: Well, you know, I can't take credit for everything.

OKB: You met him a couple of days before the interview... so that leaves us room to speculate about the connection.

NIA: Let's leave all that in the realm of urban legends.

OKB: This new phase in Malaysian opposition politics began with Mahathir suddenly turning up in court to meet your father. Did Anwar know he was coming?

NIA: Only on the day itself. But with Mahathir, you never know, you can't believe it until it actually happens.

OKB: In the pictures of that sudden meeting, I thought your father behaved very gracefully.

NIA: My father is always very graceful, that's one of his great aspects. That's him. We were not that gracious. We had to act as a bulwark against any possible derailment.

OKB: Mahathir had decided to go on, perhaps not a charm offensive, but he was moving to change the whole terrain and the first people he had to win over was your family, right?

NIA: I wouldn't call his overtures a charm offensive but he tried to engage, right?

OKB: He persisted as well.

NIA: He persisted. But it was him attending the vigil for Maria Chin Abdullah when she was detained – that illustrated some degree of commitment. And he also moved from just calling for the overthrow of Najib to calling for reforms. That was crucial.

OKB: Your family has been experiencing shock after shock to see him do this.

NIA: God moves everyone's heart, right? But at the end of the day, we will judge him from his actions. Who knows what life will impart.

OKB: Looking at his actions over the last year or so, would you say that this is Mahathir's way of saying sorry? Saying sorry does not come easily to him, so he is doing it through actions. And along the way, your family comes round to giving him the benefit of the doubt.

NIA: Some would tell me that, you know. Some would tell me that. But again, it is not only a family matter. But really, we just need to move forward, you know. There is no more time for personal grievances. I mean, why are we chosen as legislators? Why was I chosen as a wakil rakyat? It is to be focused on the agenda. You cannot keep a chip on your shoulder when you are dealing with matters of national interest.

OKB: I wish more politicians would think that way.

NIA: That's how my father brought me up.

OKB: Today, here at Penang Institute, we launched the Malay version of a book that puts forth your father as a thinker more than as a politician. Now as he is being celebrated as a political thinker, it is a good time to ask you if you see yourself as a political thinker as well.

NIA: I have a long way to go. One of the greatest prides of my life is to know that my father is a thinker, an intellectual who loves to absorb and read the ideas of philosophers, celebrates academia. That is such an important contribution as a father – I am not touching on the nation yet. It was such a beautiful thing to grow up in such an atmosphere. It enriches you in so many ways, and as I said, I have a long way to go but I continue to be inspired, I continue to learn. And for us as a nation, we have to understand the need for engagement with and celebration of these different spheres if we are to move forward.

OKB: There is really a Reformasi Generation? And that is the one now leading the charge, as it were?

NIA: And it is beautiful. We discuss the Asian Renaissance... I mean, Mahathir didn't have a vision that... I mean, his is all very, very stark. You need to have a sense of people developing their potential. Anwar has that. Malaysia has tended not to accord people their rightful place in history even if they are not victors. And that is the worst disservice you can do to the nation. Even with the Baling Talks... I mean, I condemn communism and all that, but it is important that we learn what actually happened, you know.

OKB: Yes, the details are what tell the story. Over the last two or three decades, the major leaders have been Mahathir and Anwar, right? Now you have the two of them trying to get over their falling out and coming together on the same side against all the others who came after in the establishment. Behind them, you have members of the Reformasi Generation and they are the ones pushing in the end. To me then, these older people –and that may include your father, are now a transitional group paving the way for the younger ones. I don't know if your father would think of himself that way –simply as a facilitator.

NIA: It's important to see ourselves as facilitators or enablers. You need to celebrate talent. My only concern is a lot of efforts are killed off [at source]. So much Machiavellian politicking goes on that kills off any sort of effort before it can flourish. I think that was what happened to Anwar.

OKB: Since your father was first dismissed from office and arrested in 1998, we have seen the rise of three new Malay parties. This is quite astounding. What is happening? Is Malay society maturing, splitting? What?

NIA: Time doesn't move in a vacuum. There are always players interacting. The problem we have are leaders who actively advocate through their policy and their governance, the politics of race and religion –in our education system in our curriculum, in our media, in our socialisation process. So how do you escape it? A simple example would be my children. I made sure when they were toddlers that they would go to a multicultural pre-school. That was a conscious decision. I wanted them to grow up knowing that there are people of other faiths. From there, you build further. It's a socialisation process. Solid interaction across the schools can be done but this has to come from a desire for that. There must be political will to forge a Malaysian bond. It's not being done.

OKB: I find it interesting to compare your father's party, PKR, with Mahathir's party, Parti Pribumi Bersatu Malaysia. They came about at different times for different reasons. Back in 1998, Anwar's sacking and arrest surprised him and his supporters. In fighting back, Reformasi started and PKR came into being. Taking a stance at that point required them to take a situation that is in polar opposition to that of UMNO and BN. So they adopted good governance and that line of discourse. Now, when Bersatu was formed, it did not differentiate itself by becoming a polar opposite to its opponent, UMNO. It couldn't anyway because that position is already taken by PKR. What it did was to position itself as an ideologically recognisable alternative to UMNO, and so it took the word 'Pribumi'. The point is for it to be a party that moves on a train track running alongside UMNO in order to capture voters who are discontented with UMNO. They can now leave without having to make ideological adjustments that are too painfully great. But now when PKR and PPBM do work together, they theoretically cover a very wide range of anti-UMNO sentiments. This would and should worry Najib and UMNO. Would you agree with that description of the situation?

NIA: That would be a best-case scenario. But like many things in life, success depends on being able to [convince] society. Whatever we do or think will be useless if we can't communicate it to the people, to the ground level.

OKB: The hope that many have is for Malaysians to be less and less susceptible to the politics of fear and distrust.

NIA: It all depends on the active players, on what they advocate. Time is not a vacuum; people tend to think that the march of history is forward. It does not have to be. Look at Syria, look at Saudi [Arabia]. Who could have thought that they would be more malicious and convoluted than they were five years ago. And look at America. Democracy is an active process; it's ongoing. There is no end of history, as Francis Fukuyama postulated. Democracy can provide a balance, a check on various aspects.

OKB: We now have the scenario where Mahathir and your father are on one side, and Najib and UMNO are on the other. We have a Malay-led opposition fighting a Malay-led government now. That makes identity politics a harder game to play. I see that as the significant development going into the GE14.

NIA: That would not be accurate in that in PH, there is no party dictating over the rest. In BN, UMNO dictates over the rest. PH parties have more equitable roles to play. Aesthetically, it helps [that the two coalitions are seen as Malay-led], because everyone agrees that it is the rural Malay vote that has to be targeted in terms of generating confidence and trust among the Malays. But it doesn't mean that...

OKB: But beyond just a press strategy, it does reflect something different doesn't it? You are appealing to the rural Malays to vote not based on race.

NIA: It's about overcoming the trust deficit. You have to overcome the demonisation process that BN has been carrying out [against the DAP]. Primordialism is so cliché. Do the rural Malays care that it is an MCA minister taking care of their concerns? No, because they already have overcome that doubt. They know that UMNO is dominant and no one has demonised the MCA. Give me a month of TV3 running down the MCA to the ground, I can assure you that Liow Tiong Lai [president of MCA and Transport Minister] will face a crushing defeat.

OKB: The tool to overcome that trust deficit would be the coalition? We are back to the Alliance idea, right?

NIA: Not 100 per cent. You can say maybe to 80 per cent. There has to be some improvement. I am not going to give up what I have fought for just to go back to that formula. No way. That would be a pathetic regressive movement.

OKB: It's not a bad idea –it did work for a while.

NIA: Yes, consociationalism.

OKB: But let me ask you about your family if I may. If I were a fiction writer looking at your family... I would think, 'My God, the material there!' [Laughs] I wouldn't know where to start. You got drawn into politics because of what happened to your father in 1998, you being the oldest.

NIA: My father asked me to take six months off to help with the family. And of course the six months became a year, right?

OKB: And now you are a major figure in Malaysian politics.

NIA: You see, I always thought of my father as an activist and I was among many activists. In the end, I refused to take up law because I didn't want to be a politician and all that jazz. All that helped my mental frame of mind. We all have to be a bit more humble in understanding our purpose and our role in the bigger scheme of things. Many politicians want a bigger piece of the pie, a bit of the glamour. But it's not glamorous, right? It's hard work. It's not about getting accolades. I think it is about knowing what to do and how to manage collective decisions in a very constructive manner... People dream of it as glamorous but it is about training youngsters, managing their incentives as they join politics...

OKB: I am sure it makes you feel older than you are. You are in it for good now, are you not?

NIA: What I love about it is this: I have had this chance to have such a steep learning curve. It's amazing. I wouldn't have had this opportunity to learn if it weren't for politics. I can't really complain. And I thank Mahathir's government for forcing me to go into politics. It was their transgressions against our human rights and our civil liberties that compelled me to be the politician I am today. All of us have to be in it for good, and not necessarily in one particular scope. I mean, we all have to be committed. It's not a joke anymore, you know – there is so much that is invested in this. I love my children and I want them to have as much time with their mother as possible, but I started in recent years reminding them of how important my life in politics is for their future... civic engagement. If you don't take time to explain to your children how much your work means to you, how do you expect them to accept it?

OKB: I remember a few years ago, you talked to me about wanting to start a think tank...

NIA: We are still working on it but of course nothing as flashy as Penang Institute...

OKB: From that, I see you realise how you need to have people around you to help you think.

NIA: Yes, yes. Definitely.

OKB: I just sent a selfie of you and me to my wife, who texted back the question: 'The future prime minister?' People do think of you in that way.

NIA: If only they knew the sacrifices that a prime minister has to make. I just have to think of two names, right? Yingluck Shinawatra and Benazir Bhutto.

I mean, anyone who really knows what it takes and what she is in for would definitely not be begging for that post.

OKB: History seems to be pushing you in that direction.

NIA [Laughs]: Well, whatever we can do to make things better... I have said I was a Daughter of the Reformasi and I meant it. If I had differences of opinion, I would make it heard to my father and I think that is how I am most useful – not as a blind obedient participant but as an active constructive partner in the struggle.

OKB: Well, we have had a few interactions over the years; I must say you have clearly grown into your role.

NIA: Too kind, too kind. One must read lah. Reading is important.

OKB: Thank you, Izzah, for taking the time.

35

The Diminishing of Humans Through Identity Politics[*]

Who am I?

A simple question to ask oneself and yet, no simple answer suggests itself. As long as the issue is about the singular person, it appears to be but a psychological and philosophical quandary.

Ask it in the plural and we approach what may be the key question of our times. It becomes a scrutiny of the human situation today. It becomes sociological, and it becomes highly political.

Who are we?

Now, the 'we' is the issue. In both cases, the answer can never be adequate. Much must be left out. A life is always unimaginably more than a biography can be.

In inquiring about myself, I would try to include as much as possible in my answer and in effect, I end by leaving the answer purposefully unfinished and properly tentative.

When the query is about the collective, 'Who are X?'; 'Who are Chinese?', 'Who are men?', 'Who are Malaysians?', 'Who are human beings?', one is immediately drawn to seek a neat answer that captures the essence of the collective.

This latter cognitive habit is a serious problem and whatever its roots, the fateful fault lies in mistaking denotations for connotations.

---

[*] 'Picking on the Past'; Column in *Penang Monthly*, November 2017 (earlier version published in *The Edge*, Malaysia, 25 September 2017).

When answering the self-query, I imagine different streams of experience from my past, always too many and disparate to mention. But in answering what collectives I presumably belong to, I seek to simplify instead and try to give as basic and as diminished a definition as possible.

Giving tentative, and even poetic, answers to questions about identity seems to me to be the only rational way to go. After all, is a Chinese today what a Chinese was a century ago? Is being a man today the same in Malaysia as in Thailand? Is being a man the same as being one in 1943 or even tomorrow?

Should one expect an answer about identity to be anything other than an exploratory one, then one is seeking power, and is propounding and prescribing definitions that are self-serving.

Let me illustrate this cognitive flaw, or cunning, another way.

Whenever we marry, we join fortunes with more than just a person. Whenever we make a friend, we connect with more than just an individual. This is true whether the other person belongs to our collective or not.

Whenever we think of ourselves, we explore more than just one life. Whenever we have a thought, we continue the thinking of others.

Again, the point here is that there is no clear line between the internal person and the external influences he or she continuously lives within. And since these influences and the responses to them are different for everyone, no collective identity is possible beyond the superficial. That is why we can dislike people of our own group more than we dislike members from another. That is why we can often like people of other collectives more than members of our own supposed collectives.

It is when we are encouraged to and cowed into, embracing our most superficial identities through the arousal of individual fears that we forget how we are happily and necessarily different from each other.

Now, logically, limiting such fears would be the best way for a society to avoid populism, extremism and fascism. That is perhaps the best way open to us to judge if a politician is acting in his own interests or for the good of the society he claims to represent.

What seems to characterise most developed countries is in fact the struggle to have socio-economic considerations and not identity issues, decide public policies and public discourses. Being mired in identity politics is the sign of a failing society.

Let me finish with a third way of illustrating my point. Identity politics is nothing new. This is because fear is nothing new. But when fear is allowed to run wild, as did happen in Europe in the 1930s, the paramountcy of identity politics led to some of the most unimaginable crimes being committed on those classified as essential cultural outsiders.

In fact, the shock of that period, which in effect was the culmination of centuries of the cognitive cunning that I mentioned being exercised on a global scale, was what led to the swift formulation of the Universal Declaration of Human Rights in December 1948.

The first sentence of the first article of the Declaration states that 'All human beings are born free and equal in dignity and rights.' It is a good line, simple and generic, and it intimates the despondency, the loss for words that had to follow the global human catastrophes of the decades and the centuries that preceded our times. Down to basics. A human being is a human being is a human being. Forget the rest. That is the suggested message.

Still, the cruel infancy of globalisation, the early years of quasi-social science, remain part of the world's painful legacy. So the next time we are asked 'Who are we?', we would do well to answer as tentatively as we can, if we answer at all. We would do well to ask back, 'Why? Who wants to know?' Who is it who seeks to diminish each of us?

36

The Art of
Dismantling Cultural Pluralism*

Malaysia is a special place for its natural geography and its human history but most important of all, because of its demographic complexity.

The peninsula is on the western receiving end of the wind systems of the Bay of Bengal, placed between huge and influential civilisations, and endowed as one of the world's few archipelagic regions where the climate is kind, the seas generous and where coastal cultures developed separately from but knowledgeable of each other, isolated populations traded with each other and were quietly cosmopolitan in ways that were, and are, very different from the metropolitan complexity of civilisational centres elsewhere in the world.

New actors from Europe arrived onto the scene and their orientation was much more global in reach and their capacity to transform societies and regions were much greater than those who had come before. They brought to the region what we have learned to call 'modern times'.

What this intrusion also precipitated, through the new economic structures their arrival implanted, was a hugely accelerated migration of peoples as much from within as from outside the region.

---

* 'Picking on the Past', column in *Penang Monthly*, October 2017. (Published on Merdeka Day, 31 August 2017 in *The Malaysian Insight*).

British Malaya

British Malaya, then, whether we acknowledge it today or not, created a radically new demographic situation. The intra-Nusantara population on the peninsula jumped in numbers as much as the extra-Nusantara population did. Most importantly, a new socio-economic pattern came into being, strongly tied to the emergent global economy being mid-wifed by mercantile Britain.

This global economic, political and ideological connection that accompanied and nourished the demographic changes on the peninsula is what makes Malaysia special.

It is the reason why Malaysia – and more obviously in the case of Singapore after 1963, could so easily move ahead economically after Merdeka in 1957 of its Dutch-controlled and French-controlled neighbours and the semi-colonised Thailand.

British Malaya as a whole, despite the shrewd method of indirect but effective rule used, was therefore a world quite unlike the Malay Peninsula that existed before the late eighteenth century. Let us say that the traditional 'Pax Nusantara' was replaced.

The Japanese occupation in 1942–45 was the death knell for the Pax Britannica within which British Malaya could exist and evolve so successfully. The Second World War brought a new world order into place and this sudden change exerted strong pressure on British Malaya to respond urgently and to transcend into something else that could survive in that new world order, with as little disruption and violence as possible.

What we then see after the War was a scramble, on the one hand to vainly reconstruct British Malaya and on the other to transition into a Pax Americana that for the region at that time was patently more about the Cold War than anything else.

Communalism

For the British, letting the leaders of urban Malaya take over the reins of power was the best way to ensure the defeat of communism and the continuation of its own economic and cultural influence over Malaya beyond Merdeka. And this they managed to achieve – at least until 1969.

What the British were most concerned about was not communism, which could be fought through strategic and military means. It was instead communalism that worried them.

They knew that the new and demographically diverse Malaya they had created over almost 200 years had to transcend into a new consciousness that would allow it to remain politically united and be a steady part of the capitalist global economy.

The advent of the Alliance formula stabilised by 1955 was therefore a godsend that put to rest the uncertainties that surrounded all the policies they had undertaken in the decade following their return in 1946. With Merdeka, they could more or less wipe their hands clean, and keep some of the goodies.

The incorporation of Singapore, Sabah and Sarawak in 1963 had troubles to work out but with little input from the British.

In fact, they were not told of Singapore's separation in 1965 until the very last minute. That separation, and the remaining of Sabah and Sarawak in the Federation of course were informed by communal tensions and concerns. Keeping the peace through inter-ethnic consensus was to remain the preferred formula for peace and prosperity.

All that changed in 1969.

The New Economic Policy that was put in place to solve the socio-economic problems associated with turning colonised peoples and colonial economies into a national citizenry and a national economy had great merits.

But given how finely balanced the political system had been, the heavy overall political and mentality transformation that accompanied it allowed for a new generation of Malay leaders to play a game based more on subservience than on consensus.

This transformation, aside from the NEP, included:

1. The gerrymandering that detached the population of Kuala Lumpur out of the voting process for the key state of Selangor where the rioting of 1969 had broken out.

2. The thorough muffling of free speech through constitutional amendments and other legislative measures.

3. The incorporation of almost all political parties into the Barisan Nasional coalitional system.

4. And most significantly, the promotion in practical terms of the United Malays National Organisation (UMNO) into unchallengeable prominence and dominance.

Alluring and opportunistic racialist notions such as 'Ketuanan Melayu' (Malay Supremacy) and 'Negara Islam' (Islamic State) became the preferred terms of discourse for Malay leaders within UMNO. In fact, the flaws of the former necessitated the cunning evolution into the latter.

All this has not been so much an attempt at nostalgic reference to some mythical 'Tanah Melayu' run by a people called 'Melayu' as many may think, but simply a path-dependent strategy born of the opportunistic overreaction in the early 1970s to the rioting in Selangor.

Whether that rioting was part of a coup against Tunku Abdul Rahman, I shall leave to others to decide, but the 1970s brought into being a new Malaysian polity, aided by the fact that Singapore had left and Sabah and Sarawak had remained.

As mentioned earlier, what made Malaysia Malaysia was its ethnic pluralism, but the power structure of the early 1970s allowed for the imagination to be encouraged among the Malays by their self-proclaimed race-champion, UMNO, that the country had always and shall remain 'Tanah Melayu', a land-based Malay world.

This, despite the fact that indigenous peoples of the region were always more correctly described to be living in 'Kelautan Melayu', a sea-based Malay world. The nation-state concept is most faulty when it is used to describe maritime regions.

Dismantling pluralism

Sixty years after Merdeka, then, negotiations and struggles continue to find a balance between the communities, which can make Malaysia globally significant, economically powerful and socially enviable. The notion of 'Bangsa Malaysia' championed in the prosperous early 1990s was one such attempt.

Sadly, what has been happening over the decades is that UMNO's need to keep the Malay community as captive voters also unavoidably captured the country's discourse and placed it in a perpetually contentious mode.

Once upon a time, the contention was along the dimension between inter-ethnic integration and inter-ethnic assimilation. Now it is about the degree of inter-ethnic separation.

In short, while the first decade following Merdeka was about stabilising the Alliance formula, the following six decades has seen the art of dismantling cultural pluralism being perfected.

37

No Need to Let Bigots Dictate Policy*

A nation starts building itself long before the nation-state is established. There were Germans before Germany was established and there were Italians before Italy was founded. There were definitely Malayans with a sense of being Malayans before Malaya was founded in 1957.

Where the emergence of a nation is concerned, the state tends to construct clear communal and ethnic categories with which it is able to manage and manipulate the identity building in the country. These become like Lego pieces that stick together in exact fashion but with the borders hardened. At the social everyday level, however, society builds cohesion the way one bakes a cake – the ingredients have to mix and they have to be loose, both in essence and in definition.

There is tension between these two sets of dynamics and the two have to battle for dominance. In the case of Malaysia where race and religion decide much of how its citizens describe themselves and institutionally relate to each other, there is what may be seen as a state capture of society.

Allow me to air some thoughts about some keywords first before I get down to talking about how we can limit the knee-jerk racial discrimination that infects the country.

---

* *The Edge*, Malaysia, 23 October 2017. This article is based on a speech given at the 7th Non-Discrimination Conference at the Petaling Jaya Hilton on 21 September 2017.

Some Keywords

Let's start with 'discrimination'. To 'discriminate' is a strange word. It means having the ability to notice subtle differences (which seems a positive thing), but it also means to think disapprovingly of and to act unfavourably towards things and people considered different (which is not a positive thing).

Discrimination therefore is not only about noticing a difference but also about noticing a difference deemed negative. It is hard work and it is continuous work. It is also collective work and being collective work, it easily becomes political work.

But what difference? It can't be any difference. In almost all cases, it is about difference from whatever it is one considers to be defining of oneself. We harbour no discrimination against a bird because it has wings; we harbour no prejudice against a shark because it can swim in deep waters and grow new teeth endlessly; we do not dislike a frog because it can croak. These are about elements and characteristics that we do not take on as characteristics of my selfhood.

It would therefore seem that discrimination is a self-centred cognitive process. It is about us, not about others. Others are merely tools in our efforts to find an existential comfort zone.

Then there is 'prejudice'. What is it? Well, for one thing, when one prejudges, one is technically simply being a little hasty. One is judging before one has all the facts. One is not necessarily biased; one is simply in too much of a hurry. But that is not what we mean when we say someone is prejudiced. We do not assume a time in the near future when the prejudiced person will revise his opinion based on new information; new experiences perhaps but not simply new information.

A prejudiced person is generally considered bigoted and not simply lacking in information. We ascribe malice to him, not ignorance.

Now we come 'bigotry'. The Merriam Webster dictionary defines a bigot as 'a person who is obstinately or intolerantly devoted to his or her own opinions and prejudices; especially one who regards or treats the members of a group (such as a racial or ethnic group) with hatred and intolerance'. When we think of extremists as bigots and when we do not is a question to ponder.

One last word to consider here is 'bias'. Bias simply considers emotions or processes that lead to unfair practices and results. Not much to problematise there.

Malaysian Society Today

Now let us talk about Malaysian society. Let me take a shortcut by considering the New Economic Policy. This policy was a bold move that tried to balance not only leftist and rightist thoughts. It tried to rectify historical conditions that had come to a head and these concerned long-distance immigration, hasty colonial retreats and damage control, modern economism, the emergence of nation-states and national economies from colonial bits and pieces.

In its attempt to abolish poverty, it was a leftist policy. It saw how the modern globally-connected national economy that all Malaysians had to function within was biased against some and favoured others. In that sense, it had a crude class perspective. At the same time, it was rightist in that it adopted racial categories as a central and inherent bias.

This paradox clothed the NEP's historical imperative, which was to break the connection between profession and race. It was trying to remedy the long-term effects of the augmented plural society left behind by the colonialists. And out of all that, it was hoped that nation building, state building and country building would somehow occur.

One can argue today whether we overreacted to the 1969 riots or not. After all, the fighting did take place largely in Selangor, not throughout the country; and yet, the diagnosis was for the whole diverse country and the remedy engineered to fix the problem was applied to the whole diverse population.

What was clear was that the architects of the NEP knew the gamble they were taking. Would the NEP propel the country out of its post-colonial enigmas or would the ethnocentrism it needed to encourage for the moment be triumphant in the long run? The measures were drastic but necessary, they thought; but a time limit was needed so that the patient would not die of an overdose. A twenty-year limit was thus put on the NEP.

When the NEP was thought up, religion was not considered a

national political issue and huge oil revenues had not started filling the state coffers yet. I believe these, among other factors, changed the whole equation. And so, we have ended up in a political situation that is highly divisive, that encourages ethnocentrism and that has begun to erase the nation-building accomplishments that had been made already in the final years of the British era.

We are now assumed to be a nation of defensive communities. Many of Malaysia's founding fathers did predict that communalism, more than communism, was the great enemy of the country. They were right.

But perhaps the remedy for the excessive communalism that has now taken a hard-line religious turn is not to insist on unity but to diversify diversity even more.

We have to be more discriminating. We should notice and acknowledge differences, not as differences between groups first of all but within groups. The paradox lies in us realising that the more we allow Malaysians to express their non-collective identities, the less they will feel the need to define others in order to define themselves. Embracing difference and embracing diversity come from our homes and our schools defining our young through their individual experiences and not through politically charged group images.

My cultural rights as an individual are not my ethnicity-based rights alone, whatever those are. In fact, my individual rights – and these can be clearly defined as cultural without being ethnic, are of greater importance to me and more descriptive of me than the abstract cultural or ethnic rights that others may define for me.

All a person wants, really, is not be subjected to biases all too often. And what he fears most of all is to have such biases institutionalised.

There will always be bigots but they do not have to be allowed to dictate policy. The reasons why they exert so much influence on politicians and on our public discourse are what we need to expose and to oppose.

38

What the Penang Floods Say About Malaysian Politics (and It's Not Just About Climate Change)*

Extreme Weather hits most places on Earth every now and then and recently more than ever. But when freak storms appear with an intensity stronger and more devastating than living memory can recall, it is wise to conclude that we should not take blue skies and cooling rainfalls for granted.

More obviously, governments should begin thinking very seriously about how the effects of dramatic climatic change can be mitigated at the most local level. If there is any lesson to be learned from the tropical storm that hit northern Malaysia, most notably the state of Penang on the weekend of 4–5 November, this is it.

Weather systems seem to have shifted, and the people of Penang, where the weather has almost always been mild and where disasters are queer events that take place elsewhere, were totally surprised by an extremely heavy overnight downpour accompanied by high-velocity winds that brought down dozens of trees and countless branches, onto fences, roads, houses and cars.

Seven people died.

Penang being Penang – a state defiantly run by the federal opposition since 2008, and which has for two mandate periods now

---

* *South China Morning Post*, Hong Kong, 16 November 2017.

been a poke in the eye of the powerful and long-standing central government, it has been difficult for many to consider the floods simply as a natural disaster. Instead, some schadenfreude was initially evident and fingers were pointed at the state government. But to be fair, much of this was done before most people realised how bad the situation actually was.

It did not help that there had been some flash flooding and landslides a couple of months earlier on an unprecedented scale, though a scale now dwarfed by the November storm.

A construction site landslide that took 11 lives on 21 October had further shocked the people of Penang into demanding answers and action from the Pakatan Harapan government led by Chief Minister Lim Guan Eng. His government has set up a commission of inquiry into the latter incident.

Civil society groups had been demanding for years that the state and local governments exercise more control over hillside developments.

The political pressure had therefore been mounting on Lim before the storm hit on the night of 4 November. Perhaps because of that, the chief minister was fast in responding to the latest crisis.

When natural disasters hit especially in areas usually free of them, the apparatus of the state is generally found wanting. That appeared to be the case in Penang. The floods came fast and furious in the middle of the night accompanied by winds howling like banshees, toppling trees and tearing off branches. Understandably, most services were paralysed. The extent of the crisis immobilised large parts of the island and the mainland.

Lim called for help from the military in the middle of the night and very quickly put into place a recovery plan to lessen the anxiety of many who were still shocked at how much they had lost and how suddenly.

Initial efforts taken by certain members of parliament and community leaders proved of limited use, however. Getting food and drink to the afflicted, for example, proved difficult because roads were still badly flooded and accessibility was hugely limited. But they persevered.

Steven Sim, Member of Parliament for Bukit Mertajam on the mainland side, which was perhaps the worst affected constituency, was one of those who moved quickly to bring help into flooded areas.

He said: 'The damage was so broad that getting food, and getting enough trucks together to ferry the food into the worst affected regions, proved quite impossible at first. But the sense of solidarity was immense, and we soon had someone bringing in huge amounts of newly baked bread to the victims.'

'Although the army did arrive with trucks and what not, they were not being given instructions by their commanders to get into the thick of things.'

What turned the tide, as it were, in bringing aid to the thousands afflicted by the waters that rose as high as 12 feet, was the quick response of the community. Aid soon came from across Malaysia, donated by generous Malaysians and brought in by concerned and compassionate individuals. Volunteers appeared from near and far, some coming up from Johor, the southernmost state on the peninsula. The speed at which debris was cleared away and houses and streets washed clean was astounding, a testimony to how Penangites and Malaysians rose to the occasion to help their fellow citizens.

However, it would not be Malaysia if the flood disaster were not politicised. Deputy Prime Minister Ahmad Zahid Hamidi considered the occasion a time of political opportunity, and thinking that the disaster had hurt the standing of the Penang government, said that the floods were 'a sign from God that the state was ripe for the taking'.

The disaster also took place while the Malaysian parliament was in the middle of its debate over the federal budget. To a question from a Penang member of parliament on whether the federal government intended to use resources from its contingency fund to aid Penang's flood victims, the Minister in the Prime Minister's Department, Shahidan Kassim, said the opposition's criticism of the budget proposal as a whole was a rejection of potential federal aid and the federal opposition was therefore not in support of aid to those victims.

Such quaint logic notwithstanding, in the aftermath of the aid efforts mounted by all and sundry, and after all the relief centres had been closed, it appears that the Penang state government despite certain clear weaknesses concerning its overall ability to act in a crisis, gained much sympathy for its overall compassionate handling of the situation. The tremendous solidarity shown by common folk and by volunteers of all colours and persuasions under their watch – notwithstanding some reports of dishonest individuals pretending to be victims in order to obtain donated items – is a credit to Malaysians in general and is not something to be scoffed at.

The fact remains though that islands are the frontline victims of climate change and for a small and hilly island like Penang, environmental management and developmental prudence will hopefully become an increasingly important consideration in the policymaking of the state government, as it has to be for all governments today.

39

This is the Moment of Truth for Malaysia's Race-based Politics[*]

After all the analysing done by pundits on Malaysia's political dynamics in the post-Mahathir period, the country has now come to the strange point of being in a potential pre-Mahathir period.

There is now the more-than-theoretical possibility that 92-year-old former Prime Minister Mahathir Mohamad will return to lead the country, should the opposition coalition win the coming general election. Though unlikely, the chances of that happening are not exactly slim.

In many ways, Malaysia has been locked in a period of transition for two decades. One could say this was triggered by the Reformasi movement in 1998 when the country's two top leaders fell out with each other and behind that, by the socio-economic travails ignited by the Asian Financial Crisis; or one could claim that it began with Mahathir's retirement in October 2003; or that it started with the surprising results of the 2008 elections when the ragtag opposition managed on election night to win five of the 13 states.

Behind these unending trends lies the fact that a new generation of young leaders – some inspired by the 1998 protests but most thrust into the limelight in 2008, have been waiting impatiently to take over but are still playing merely a supporting role, not only because the old leaders are still active but also because of the solidity of the discursive and economic domination of the ruling Barisan Nasional coalition over the rural population in particular.

---

[*]   *South China Morning Post*, Hong Kong, 6 December 2017.

Then there was the advent of Internet news media, a prominent milestone of which was the founding of the Malaysiakini news website in 1999. This was followed a decade later by The Malaysia Insider (brought to its knees by political pressure in 2016 and since resurrected as The Malaysian Insight) and by other websites. Social media also appeared after the turn of the century to act as an effective new tool for political activism.

Where the opposition parties are concerned, we have seen its major coalitions evolve from the Barisan Alternatif in 1999 to Pakatan Rakyat in April 2008 to Pakatan Harapan in 2015, which since then has evolved to include two newly formed Malay-based parties: Parti Amanah Negara (splintered from the Islamist Parti Agama SeMalaysia, or PAS) and Mahathir's Parti Pribumi Bersatu Malaysia (consisting of UMNO dissidents).

How you can be sure the Malaysian election date will be...

The dominant United Malays National Organisation (UMNO) has in the meantime gone through its own transformation, taking more and more conservative racial and religious stances the more its defences crumble, which they did in 2008 and 2013. Abdullah Badawi's huge popularity in 2004 dissipated surprisingly quickly and his replacement Najib Razak, the present prime minister, went from being much more popular than his party at the time of his rise to power to being a big burden to its reputation today.

Transitions that go on and on are of course not really transitions any more. Instead, they define the new normal, if for no other reason, then surely by virtue of the fact that the status quo has over time managed to dig itself in. Malaysian politics in the twenty-first century is now best described as a state of trench warfare.

How, or if, this will end any time soon is the big question.

The return of Mahathir in politics should thus be of the greatest interest to Malaysianists. What are the dangers that Mahathir, a man who has been at the heart of Malaysian politics since the 1960s, sees in the Najib administration which brought this nonagenarian out of retirement so fully that he would form a new party, bring it into the fold of the opposition coalition and manoeuvre himself into the chair of this body? Why does he eat humble pie the way he has done, and approach Anwar Ibrahim, the man he so mercilessly sacked in 1998 and put in jail, for rapprochement? Why has he been traversing and crisscrossing the country, with his faithful and aged wife in tow, whipping up dissent against Najib, the son of the man who brought him in from the cold in 1972?

Few know more than him how UMNO politics and Malaysian governance have relied on dubious processes covering corruption, political patronage, vote manipulation, mass media control and draconian laws. What is different now?

The fact that he calls his new party a 'Pribumi' party, highlighting the fact that it is a Malay-based party, is key to understanding what the situation in Malaysia is today, at least to his mind. Bersatu is also a race-based party that immediately and paradoxically wishes to go into coalition with Pakatan Harapan, whose expressed concerns are about good governance and not racial one-upmanship, and in which the Democratic Action Party (DAP), long dubbed by UMNO as an anti-Malay Chinese-chauvinist party, is a founding partner.

The Malaysian economy is turning. Will Najib's luck follow suit?

Within that nascent coalition are three de facto Malay-based parties, the other two being Amanah and Anwar Ibrahim's Parti Keadilan Rakyat. For the coming elections, these are arrayed alongside the DAP against UMNO, the major Malay-based party, surrounded by its weaker or neutered Barisan Nasional allies and tentatively supported by the Islamist PAS.

No wonder there is talk about a pending Malay voter tsunami against the federal government in the coming elections. The time seems to have come when the Malay community has to deal with the long-term negative consequences of UMNO's Malay-centrism on Malaysian nation-building. The economic burdens on the lower classes are heavy while national economic figures remain positive, and UMNO governs in the face of four Malay parties in opposition to it. (No doubt PAS seems more willing to put in its lot with UMNO than with the others).

One big definite change over the last few decades has been the emergence of a large enough educated urban Malay middle class whose members appreciate the social stability and cultural pride that only good governance can bring instead of acting out of highly augmented fear of economic and political irrelevance as a community.

The Bumiputra policy was never supposed to be a goal in itself. In fact, the success of Malay-centric nation-building requires Malaysian nation-building to remain successful. It is here, I believe, that Mahathir's dilemma lies. Malay-centrism alone will get the Malays nowhere. As a slogan, Malay-centrism rings hollow if the country becomes ever more divided, the poorer classes become ever poorer and nothing in its present trajectory promises stronger reasons for national pride in the immediate future.

Reforming Malay politics into a shape that accepts the multiculturalism that so clearly marks Malaysian society and that recognises the challenges the digital age poses seems to be the goal for Mahathir and many others. There is real fear that Malay-centrism a la UMNO has lost the plot and acting in denial of this fact is dragging the Malay community – and the country as well – into a political black hole.

40

We are Equal Only Through Our Vote[*]

Freedom cannot be understood apart from power. Like with all good dichotomies, it is never clear where the one turns into the other or lives off the other.

Today, it is a staple in management courses and sloganeering to talk about empowering employees. 'Empower' is also a term used from below. Empowering minorities, empowering women and empowering the poor all sound fine because we assume an extreme victimhood among these groups.

We do not talk as easily about empowering those who are already in positions of power or those who are obviously not victims of someone else's power. We do that only in relation to a bigger power that they have to suffer. We do not, logically, talk about empowering somebody who has absolute power and only do that when it comes to those who very weak. Those who are not very weak, we do not consider empowering too much for fear that they quickly become suppressors in turn.

After all, we do assume someone or some group having the power to empower others. Thus, an authoritarian cannot logically be empowered further, at least within his realm.

From this, we see that Freedom and Power have arms locked, conceptually. Freedom has a context and that context is the inevitable contest for relative power. That is why we consider the notion and

---

[*] *The Edge*, Malaysia, 25-31 December 2017. Reprinted in *Penang Monthly*, February 2018.

the institutionalising of checks and balances to be so important. It is wrong to think of it simply as the result of democratic thinking. The Magna Carta, seen by Anglo-Saxon thinkers as the starting shot for the curbing of the powers of the English monarch was a check on the king and a balancing of powers between his house and those of the nobles. Nothing very democratic there.

What it did show was that absolute power carries its own demise within itself, in that it leads to revolt at some level, and so, to protect the status quo, power must be curbed and shared among a few.

The point to remember is that power is not shared, and cannot be shared, equally among all within the realm. That would in fact be tantamount to the dissolving of power altogether, which we know is not a stable or possible situation. Power will instantaneously rise again the way warlords arose the minute a Chinese dynasty fell. Thus, even in the most developed of democracies, the only power shared by all is the vote. Beyond the vote and after the vote, the contestation for power begins and never ends.

Nevertheless, it is with the free and fair vote that a democratic culture comes into being. That is how notions of fairness penetrate society and bring dignity to its politics. The integrity of its vote is the measure of a society's self-esteem.

But then, the value of the singular vote can be, and is, easily diminished or even nullified through the electoral structure. That is why the construction of an electoral system is such a science in itself. Keeping this construction a technocratic and fair process is a gargantuan task though since the parties wishing to load the electoral dice are always present and fight to command the proceedings.

Gerrymandering and malapportionment of constituencies, which are rampant and par-for-the-course in the case of Malaysia do make elections farcical to a painful degree. When you compromise the egalitarian vote, you compromise the legitimacy of the system and you damage the reputation of the country. Worse than that, you open a Pandora's Box of corruption, arrogance, unaccountability and non-transparency.

Power is thus something a society needs to systemically check and limit. Freedom after the vote, equality after the vote, depends on the fairness of the electoral system for it is with that perceived and experienced fairness that society heals itself.

A healthy balance between the freedom of the individual and the power of the state lies therefore in making and keeping the electoral system free and fair for it is there the ethos and pathos of the population are kept focused and dignified. How this can be done, how the Pandora's Box can be closed (relatively, in any case) is through the exercise of individual freedom – through self-empowerment, if you like.

Freedom is as Freedom Does

Some of you may still remember the film Gandhi. There are two scenes in there that are still clear in my mind after all these years.

One is where Mahatma Gandhi told a distraught Hindu man who had just lost his child in violent rioting between Hindus and Muslims that to redeem himself, he should adopt a child, but that child must be a Muslim. What he was suggesting to this poor man was that if he wished to break the cycle of racial killings, of racist intent, he should act the way a non-racist would.

There is another episode, a famous one, where Gandhi, after much contemplation and strategising, hits upon the plan to defy British rule by acting as if it did not exist. So he and a small of band of followers set off on 12 March 1930, on a long march, over 240 miles across western India. This took time, of course and news of the march spread and more joined so that they altogether got to the sea and started making salt. With that magic act, the hegemony of the British Raj began crumbling, at least for those who participated. Those watching would also soon, in the subsequent violence used by the British against the demonstrators, witness cracks in colonialism's hegemonic wall.

Now, this salt march is often described as an act of non-violent mass resistance. I see it simply as the gaining of freedom in one fell swoop through the power of the free act, just like the way a fair judge can bring immediate justice with one just sentence. The salt march was a self-empowering denial – and an ignoring – of coercive power.

Freedom thus boils down to being the free act itself. Freedom is as freedom does. Freedom is not given, it is taken.

41

Why the Opposition Has a Shot at Toppling the Barisan Nasional with Mahathir at the Helm*

Malaysia's parliament will be dissolved sometime during the first half of 2018. That is a legal certainty. The general election that is to follow within two months after that will be the third to be held since Dr Mahathir Mohamad retired as prime minister in October 2003.

It will also be one where the 93-year-old doctor will attempt to become prime minister again, now that the opposition has named him their pick for the top job should they emerge victorious.

A Declaration of War

Even if he does not succeed in this audacious attempt, what Mahathir has managed to do after leaving UMNO is nothing short of astounding. Mahathir's sense of strategy is clearly as sharp as it has always been and one should certainly not underestimate his reading of the political dynamics of the country today.

This is a man with his finger on the pulse of Malaysian politics. Like a master chess player, he left the tournament circuit in 2003 before he could be defeated.

Now he returns, a wild card that makes it into the finals.

It is not so much Najib Razak that the opposition coalition Pakatan Harapan is trying to unseat. It is UMNO. This is important.

---

* *ChannelNewsAsia*, Commentaries, 8 January 2018.

At this point in time, Najib is less popular than the party he leads. In that sense, the prime minister is living off the glory of the party's earlier days and the Malaysian public's memory of its old accomplishments.

Resigning from UMNO was the first step Mahathir took following his largely ineffective criticism against Najib's administration from within the party. He had also resigned in 2008 when Abdullah Badawi was prime minister but rejoined when Najib took over in 2009.

A resignation by Mahathir is not a throwing in of the towel but a declaration of war.

What is vitally different this time around is that Mahathir has not only given up on UMNO, deeming it to be beyond redemption.

He has also managed to make common cause with the opposition, which over the last decade has shown itself to be a plausible countervailing force to the ruling coalition, the Barisan Nasional led by UMNO.

Waiting to Strike

A master strategist is one who waits and strikes, and then waits again for the next opportunity. As Najib came under pressure from within and without in recent years and as he acted against his attorney-general, his deputy prime minister and other UMNO leaders, Mahathir knew to pick up the pieces and was soon able to spring a surprise on the world.

His next strategic step was to found a new party, and so, Parti Pribumi Bersatu Malaysia (PPBM) was officially established on 7 September 2016. Fifteen months down the road, on 29 December 2017, that party managed to hold its first annual general assembly.

It is equally telling that this new party was not created to be a racially inclusive one. Not only did Mahathir make PPBM a Malay party like UMNO, even if it does allow non-Malay associate members – the uniform chosen for its annual general meeting (AGM) was red, the traditional colour seen at UMNO AGMs.

Both concretely and symbolically, PPBM is challenging UMNO on UMNO's home turf.

Whatever other principles Mahathir may live by, he knows that to win in politics as in chess, you need more than kings, queens, bishops, knights and castles. You also need foot soldiers. And you need a constituency.

Mahathir is no Don Quixote. He does not fight for the sake of fighting. He fights to win and before striking, he identifies his enemy's weak points even as he strengthens his allies.

The alternative discourses of multiracialism and good governance are campaign narratives that have been captured effectively by other opposition parties such as the Democratic Action Party (DAP) and by Anwar Ibrahim's Parti Keadilan Rakyat (PKR). So another Malay-led multiracial party is not likely to win over any new body of voters. In fact, it would only lead to further internal contest among opposition parties.

So the voters to gun for are UMNO's more devoted supporters, plain and simple.

Picking up the Pieces

This is what Mahathir knows to bring to the table. Indeed, his moves to win over his old enemy, Anwar Ibrahim and his supporters, is a study in masterful strategy.

Despite being the sworn enemy of the opposition for so long, Mahathir went on a charm offensive to convince the opposition forces arrayed around Anwar, originally to fight Mahathir himself, that the future of Malaysian politics depends on them working together.

This he has managed to do, partly because the opposition leaders were at their wits' end after Najib managed to lure Parti Agama SeMalaysia (PAS) to his side, acceding step-by-step in the process to a conservative Islamic agenda.

This is not an easy game to master and in going down that path, Najib may have pleased conservative segments of the Malay population but he has upset many others at the same time including some of the sultans and many older civil servants. These provided more pieces for Mahathir to pick up. Not all are for the picking, no doubt, especially the monarchs whom Mahathir badly affronted during the 22 years he was prime minister.

Anwar's PKR and the coalition that he had built could only go so far and win only that much support. The biggest hurdle the now-defunct Pakatan Rakyat faced was the unwillingness within key segments of the Malay community to ditch UMNO. UMNO to them is synonymous with the Malays' special position and has been seen, rightly or wrongly, as the protector of Malay culture.

Calling for good governance can only attract a certain segment of Malay voters. What Mahathir realises is that although Malay support may shift away from UMNO on the issue of good governance, it can do that only to a limited extent. And that limit has been reached.

In this context, racial appeal is also needed. What PKR stands for, associated as strongly as it is to the DAP, is too vague and detached from the daily lives of many Malay voters especially those in more rural settings. With PPBM as a key member of Pakatan Harapan, the coalition's ability to appeal to the Malay community has been strongly enhanced.

Mahathir then went the extra mile at his new party's first AGM and apologised publicly for his past wrongdoings. His strategy to place himself at the head of the opposition and to be its prime ministerial candidate has now been amazingly secured.

Furthermore, the agreement within Pakatan Harapan to commence legal proceedings to obtain a pardon for Anwar has softened resistance to Mahathir heading the opposition.

How sincere Mahathir's remorse is and whether he can reconcile genuinely with old enemies in the opposition are not the issues here. Dissociating the Malay community's interests from UMNO's party interests in the minds of rural Malays is the issue and for that, it is the key to toppling the Barisan Nasional.

To what extent Mahathir's leadership of the opposition succeeds in doing that will be given an irrefutable answer in the exciting general election to be held later this year.

42

Spiralling Back Towards Reformasi[*]

The return of former prime minister Tun Dr Mahathir Mohamad to the forefront of Malaysian politics at the age of 92 – 19 years after he sacked his deputy Datuk Seri Anwar Ibrahim and 14 years after he retired as prime minister – is astounding not only in a Guinness Book of World Records kind of way but also because of some interesting things it articulates about Malaysian politics in the twenty-first century.

Foremost is the apparent stagnated political transition that the country is caught in. The reformasi or reform movement that Anwar got off the ground in September 1998 captured the imagination of Malaysians and brought forth a generation that did not share the fears instilled in their forebears by the consensual nature of inter-ethnic Malaysian politics. This generation of Malaysians did not buy the conservative 'this is as good as it gets' idea nor did they think that the only way to discuss politics was to tiptoe around the most difficult subjects. That much Anwar managed to inspire.

Although the movement was partially headed by older leaders, the impetus came from the young and youthful – and these included those who went into politics then, those who now write for the new media and on social media and those who voted for the newly energised opposition coalition.

And so, even if the leader of the opposition today is in his nineties, he should not be seen as a symbol of or a throwback to the politics of the pre-reformasi era. Societies are never stagnant and politics can,

---

[*] Appeared as 'Back to Reformasi' in *The Edge*, Malaysia, 29 January–4 February 2018.

therefore, not be unchanging. And even if a transitional period appears stagnant, it nevertheless is spiralling off in a certain direction.

And it is that direction that needs to be identified and named. Malaysia in 2018 is not the same as Malaysia in 1998. And even if many of the leading names are from an earlier period, the battle is not the same one.

After the 'tsunami' in 2008 gave five states to the opposition, the Barisan Nasional failed to recover and instead weakened further in 2013, when it lost the popular vote. The coming fourteenth general election is, therefore, understandably seen by many as a new arrangement of reformasi forces bent on toppling the UMNO-led BN. This time around, it has the man that the reformasi movement once saw as its arch-enemy, Mahathir, as its frontman.

This paradox needs explaining and part of that explanation is found in the fact that while all previous opposition coalitions since 1990 had included PAS, this time it does not. This difference is highly significant.

After the excesses of the later period of the Mahathir government, the Tun Abdullah Ahmad Badawi administration chose to define itself when it took office at the end of 2003 through a reform agenda. Abdullah was in effect stealing Anwar's thunder and it worked. He captured over 90 per cent of the parliamentary seats in the 2004 election.

It was also important to Abdullah to expound a new perspective on the role of religion as well – his Islam Hadhari idea. As his reforms proved ineffectual, voters turned against him in 2008. By April 2009, a 'coup' had been launched within UMNO against Abdullah. Datuk Seri Najib Razak took over and he understood the times well enough to adopt the term 'Transformation' to replace Abdullah's 'Reform'.

He also attempted to popularise the term 'One Malaysia', which tried to reflect Mahathir's impressively successful 'Bangsa Malaysia' from the 1990s. Sadly for the country, Najib's term now carries very negative connotations worldwide.

Strongly disappointed by weak voter support in 2013, Najib appeared to switch strategy from trying to gain the middle ground to strengthening his hold on BN and its core constituencies. By courting

PAS, he managed to break up the opposition Pakatan Rakyat. This use of religion – something Abdullah realised he had to do, which Najib did not consider during his first term in power – succeeded beyond what he could have hoped for. But it came at a huge price.

It led to splits not only in PAS, which was expected, but in UMNO as well. The dissent in UMNO and the reasons for that dissent appear at least to be twofold. One is the 1Malaysia Development Bhd scandal that rocked the administration and dented Malaysia's international reputation significantly and the other is the central government's encouragement of Islamist tendencies and tolerance of Malay-centric racism.

It also led to Mahathir becoming UMNO's blood enemy.

The fourteenth general election has been identified as a do-or-die situation by many pundits. This is because it is difficult for them to imagine that the country will remain the same whoever the winner turns out to be. Should the opposition win, then, of course, great changes are expected to come. But even if BN manages once again to retain a majority in Parliament, that success – that narrow escape, as some would definitely think it to be – should precipitate harsh measures aimed at consolidating the coalition's power.

Since the 2013 election, the federal government has in many ways been acting the way one may expect an administration under great duress to act. The sense of mission that is so vital to a developing nation is no longer felt and certainly not in the way it was felt in the 1990s. In its place is a sense of entrenched warfare.

In its search to rejuvenate itself, the reformasi movement now strangely finds itself in need of Mahathir's strategic skills and sense of national purpose to accomplish – come to power and reform the system of government. And even if the leaders continue to be from another age, the stage cannot but be soon taken over by much younger players. Many are already standing in line. Whether we like it or not, time is always on the side of the young.

43

Individual Freedom Is a Matter of National Survival*

A New Era is upon us. This is no longer a controversial statement as far as I can gather. Indeed, it is a boring truism by now. A new page in our already speedy times has been turned and it is defined geo-economically by the rise of China and of India and it is noted in how different societies are elbowing their way to get ahead in the queue.

More concretely put, it is the sum of the exponentially-driven consequences of electronic innovations that began not very long ago. And, as with all new eras, we were already mired in it before we noticed it. As has often been remarked upon, the smartphone as we know it today, which now controls our day, is only 11 years old. WhatsApp, with which you organise your contact network, is nine years old, as is Airbnb. And yes, the ride-hailing app Uber is eight years old and Malaysia's incredibly successful Grab app is only two years younger.

Your children's current favourite app, Instagram, may have taken a while to take off properly but it is, nevertheless, only seven or eight years old.

In this company, Facebook is really old, launched as it was in February 2004. Twitter isn't much younger. Its first proper prototype began working in the spring of 2006. You can see why teenagers consider Facebook and Twitter apps for the old. And Skype ... I

---

* *The Edge*, Malaysia, 26 February–4 March 2018.

haven't heard that platform mentioned in quite a while but that could be because it is even older than Facebook – by a whole year.

What all this tells us is that the disorientation you currently feel in your daily life is totally rational. You should feel that way and you have every right to feel that way. In fact, you can take comfort in the fact that your younger peers, who boast of their prowess in handling communication devices and apps today, will soon feel the way you do right now. They will also be bypassed.

The pace of IT development today is exponentially increasing, while our human ability to sync to it individually is highly limited, often restricted by the socio-political culture, educational exposure and of course, the communicative habits of the society we live in.

Despite Malaysia's once-glorious stature as one of Asia's flying geese, it is today more like a floundering duck. 2020 is only two years away and Malaysians definitely do not feel any uplifting wind beneath their wings.

Any business consultant today will tell you that technical innovativeness, outside-the-box thinking and mental bravado are what you need to stay competitive – all that seems reasonable enough advice to an individual. Be brave, be smart, be receptive. But individuals need collective conditions to excel and that is what we should be looking at.

Science and technology have reached a point where their impact has gone ballistic. That is one way of describing Industrialisation 4.0. Which societies seem to be answering the call to be IT-smart and be confident well? If you ask me, one of them is definitely Sweden.

Several points are worth noting about a small advanced country like Sweden in this context. Its welfare system was developed in the shadow of Western capitalism on one side and communism on the other. With the end of the Cold War, this country of nine million people – with winters that last half a year – had to re-orientate itself politically and economically, though no doubt leveraging certain aspects of its earlier accomplishments. It is now a leader in globally relevant technical innovations.

First, the scientific rationality of Swedish society is a higher valued good and their children are taught to think scientifically on all matters. Second, the welfare system though curbed since the days of the Cold War, has created a mentality that considers keeping the income gap small to be a prerequisite for social harmony and as a matter of justice.

Third, unlike Malaysia, where class analyses have been discouraged since the 1950s, Sweden has in post-war times preferred to use concepts of class instead of race and religion in its political contestations. Fourth, its democratic culture has not feared freedom of speech the way most Asian societies do. Freedom of the press, which over time has developed a relatively high standard of journalism has kept the fear of arbitrary power – which is the common condition of tyranny – at bay.

And fifth, feminism is an evidently empowering force in Swedish society. If half the population feels suppressed, then one should not expect society itself to feel free.

In the end, the point I am making is that we need to think of individual freedom as a socially created condition. A person cannot be free if his fellows are not. Freedom is a collective condition.

But I am really not talking about political philosophy. I am really talking about modern economics. If innovativeness is what will save a society, then individual freedom on a national scale is the best way to generate that. Embracing technological developments and reacting effectively to them, especially now when innovations happen at lightning speed will require a society that produces bold, confident and scientifically minded young people of all genders.

Freedom from fear is the strategy for survival.

44

Why Meet the Twenty-first Century with Twentieth Century Mindsets?*

We should not forget that in the days before social media and news websites, the flow of information – basically through schools and through daily newspapers, television and radio stations, was highly centralised and easily controlled.

Then came the 1990s and the Internet took over our lives in a big way, and with it a blogging culture began to flourish. For Malaysia, it coincided with the disastrous 1997–98 Asian Financial Crisis.

This democratisation of communication – and knowledge – accelerated with the coming of social media. SMSes, Facebook, Twitter, WhatsApp and Instagram, among other developing technologies provided everyone with the means to express themselves from below and to access news sites not controlled by the government.

The search engine revolution has given us immediate access to most facts, sweeping aside the rows of encyclopaedias and dictionaries in our homes.

Hypertext allows us to connect ideas in ways we could not before.

The development of the smartphone only a decade ago has taken the liberating of the individual from his or her immediate surroundings to a whole new level. The preferred apps and the preferred settings on his or her smartphone now decide and define the flow of information and the lines of communication.

---

* Editorial, *Penang Monthly*, March 2018.

We can now choose our own news, our own threads of thought and our own special collection of 'friends' and contacts. And we can now rant and gripe and believe anything that our individual socio-cultural situation, our personal history and our own level of knowledge prone us to do.

This opening of the mind is something strongly positive, no doubt. It empowers people. But as with all mass empowerment, it has led to a fragmentation of collective values and a decentralisation of public discourses – and also to governments losing whatever ability and coercive power over knowledge that it had had to imbue the majority of its citizens with a sense of common causes.

Keeping the World Twittered

How governments and how governing in general adapt to this, is a subject for immediate research. American President Donald Trump's twisted tweet communication with the world can be understood merely as an old man's way of awed handling – and retreating from – a world technologically changed beyond his recognition and holding that changing world hostage in the process.

For Malaysian society at large, what accompanies the excitement over social media and new media is, first off, the mass disillusionment and anger over being tricked and being kept in the dark for decades by the mass media of old and the governments that controlled them. It has become clear to Malaysians that their sense of their own history had been played with and their multiple identities warped, categorised and politicised in a slow-boil process beyond recognition.

This realisation has generated a deep cynicism among Malaysians which alternative nascent collective discourses and attempts at opposition politics cannot really bridge. The generational shifts in reality have been moving too fast for that to happen.

What we have ended up with is a country that is in denial over its own fragmentation. No doubt the cultural diversity had always made common causes difficult to reach an agreement on, but the diversity today is greater than and transcends these ethnic and religious divisions.

The present political miscellany in the Malay community, whose majority status increases on a day-to-day basis along with its internal income gap is a clear sign of this general fragmentation in thought, social and economic orientation.

Put another way, the communications technologies that have brought such profound and disruptive changes to Malaysia's shores are part and parcel of the new industrialisation tsunami sweeping the world. It is disastrous therefore for a country today to still play power games built on the nineteenth and twentieth-century defensive mechanisms we call nationalism and identity politics and maintain an education system that is still trying to solve problems formulated in the 1950s.

The new world that is upon us is a time of opportunity as well as of disruptions. It all depends on how creatively and light-footedly Malaysians can re-describe themselves as a people of the future and not of times past.

45

A Final Quarrel Between a Repentant Grandfather and Old-fashioned Self-absorbed Parents*

As the fourteenth general election draws near, the sense that Malaysia – and the whole Asia-Pacific region, for that matter, must now leap into a new era is growing stronger by the day.

What seems common to advanced countries and developing countries alike is the need for governments to realise that profound disruptions caused by the digital revolution are already happening. Their old ways of doing things and the old structures created for doing those things are now the greatest hindrance to the country's ability to take full advantage of the opportunities offered by the Fourth Industrial Revolution.

And so, where Malaysia is concerned, much courage is needed to discard the old ways of thinking that have become inhibitive and to dismantle the structures created by those old ways of thinking which now stand in the way of new strategies that suit latecomers like Malaysia.

Yes, Malaysia is a latecomer – not so much in that it started late, but in it has been a great waster of time and opportunity. And how has it been wasting time and opportunity? Answering that question is what requires courage, because it is necessarily a radical act and it is

---

* Editorial, *Penang Monthly*, April 2018.

necessarily a dangerous stance because it threatens the survival of the old structures.

The South-East Asian nations founded after the Second World War began building their state apparatus, their national identity and their national economy in response to domestic tensions and external pressures. Whatever their individual solutions were, these are now from another age. Had they been successful, they would have achieved a stable and free society and made themselves largely redundant.

As with good parenting, which fosters children so that they can manage the future on their own, a nation-builder succeeds by nurturing the nation and the citizenry towards maturity. Once that is achieved, governments should merely play a supportive role to help citizens excel, just as parents of young adults should dismantle the barriers that they placed in the way of the children when they were children.

This seldom happens though. We notice it in how schoolchildren in the US recently had to take matters into their own hands against the passion of their elders for guns.

Now, let's go back to Malaysia and the coming general election. The Malaysian citizen is now grown, ready and eager to test his wings, but it is the parents – in the form of old conflicts, old authoritarianism and old notions of race and nation-building – who refuse to let him leave home to take on an exciting world that they understand better than the aged parents. The future is their challenge to face, not the parents'. But bad parents tend to want their children to live at home forever.

This is why the notion of Malaysia being in a transition is so strong among young Malaysians today. The need to take matters into their own hands is getting undeniably strong. Some of them are escaping out the window or the backdoor, some are arguing among themselves in the living room, some are sulking and will not come out of the toilet, some won't eat the bland food they are fed every day and some are in the bedroom planning revolt. The parents, in turn, have the front door sealed, the Wi-Fi turned off and the TV locked on one single channel; and they have employed religious bouncers at the gate to keep everyone locked in. The home is now a prison for the young spirit.

In this scenario, one could poignantly and pointedly say that the system's grandfather, Tun Dr Mahathir Mohamad, seems to have realised the error of his own ways and has now come out of retirement to help end the confinement of Malaysia's future generations.

46

Outraged Enough to Go Vote or Cynical Enough to Stay Home?*

The world may be stunned by the enormity of national scandals that have hit Malaysia and further dazed by the flippant official explanations that accompany them. Yet, the ruling BN remains expressly confident of victory in the coming elections. A high enough voter turnout, however, can cause an upset.

So many bizarre and inconceivable things have happened in recent years to damage Malaysia's international reputation and self-image that, for a mortified and embarrassed public, a change of government at the federal level no longer carries the deep sense of incredulity and anguish that it once had. In fact, many now consider the coming general election to be a do-or-die contest – deep institutional reforms must take place if the many negative and speedily converging trends are to be reversed.

Should the Opposition coalition under former prime minister Tun Dr Mahathir Mohamad win in 2018, then some serious investigations into these scandals are unavoidable and most of the reforms it now promises are likely to be carried out in the months that immediately follow.

But should the BN under Prime Minister Datuk Seri Najib Razak triumph despite the outrageous scandals that surround it – the continuing high level of national debt; the apparent incompetence and callousness of many of its leaders; and the rising cost of living, among

---

* Cover story, *Penang Monthly*, April 2018.

a list of other problems – many expect a crackdown on civil liberties and on recalcitrant individuals to take place quickly.

Being made the laughing stock of the world is one thing but rising prices and the dramatic fall in value of the ringgit hurts working families more immediately – and that does not put anyone in a forgiving mood.

In fact, people are in a very bad mood in Malaysia today, to such an extent that feeling helpless, outraged and ignored may turn out to be a stronger impulse to act than the tried and tested issue of race and religion.

Tellingly, for the Opposition to reuse an old slogan and simply call for change today as it did so effectively in 2008 and 2013 now seems rather unimaginative and dull – and even glib. The fact is, much has been changing in Malaysian society over the last five years and young Malaysians today are very different from those of a generation ago. Most obviously, they are not as cowed as their parents were.

Excitingly and significantly, with the Malay community unprecedentedly represented by five parties now – and the doors of the Chinese-based multiracial DAP also opened to them, attempts by the status quo to control voter behaviour are not likely to succeed as well as they did before.

An Outmoded Superstructure

In fact, the status quo now refers only to the political superstructure. The socioeconomic reality in Malaysia has been shifting for years. Urbanisation has reached the Malay community in a big way: the control of information that the central government once had is now largely undermined; the unquestioning identification of the young with the political habits of their elders, be the latter of their own community or not is greatly weakened; and the globalising of education, friendship and work opportunities has made new ideas easily obtainable, old ideas easily dismissed and collective identities multitudinous.

There are many possible scenarios for a post-GE14 Malaysia.

No doubt, the denial of its traditional parliamentary two-thirds majority since 2008 and the loss of the popular vote in 2013 have not only shaken up the ruling coalition; they have also destroyed the shroud of invincibility that it had enjoyed since 1969. That shroud is not some invisible garment. It is woven from concrete measures undertaken over the years to benefit the ruling coalition, such as malapportionment and gerrymandering of seats; control over the mass media; racial and religious rhetoric; and the dubious use of draconian legislation, among other things. Furthermore, the advantages of incumbency at the federal level are often based on the questionable use of huge sums of money to buy votes and to finance BN candidates.

One often noted pattern in Malaysian politics has been that one strong BN election would be followed by a weak one. This pattern was clearly broken in 2013 when the weak showing by BN in 2008 was followed by an even weaker one. The new pattern now is one where the BN is expected to lose some ground in every successive election. It would appear today that Tun Abdullah Ahmad Badawi's failure in 2003–2009 to reform the regime convinced many Malaysians that BN – and UMNO, is inherently unable to reform itself. Mahathir, who retired in October 2003 after 22 years as prime minister and who had been actively involved in Malay politics since just after the Second World War, is definitely convinced of this.

For many, he is on a last-ditch campaign to right not only his own wrongs but the wrongs of a regime left without any check-and-balance mechanism – and that regime has arrived at that unhappy point through blind and excessive use of identity politics to the detriment of the state apparatus, national identity and the national economy, just to mention a few key areas. The level of Malaysian education, just to name another example, is another area where the standard has dropped from what was once an enviable level in the region, to an appallingly low degree. This in itself is an unforgivable crime committed on the future generations of Malaysians.

Equally serious is the damage that has been done to the judiciary and to the Malaysian civil service, which was once highly respected throughout the region.

The pattern continues and sorely shows why the call for 'reformasi', however vague it may have been at times, was a deeply necessary one. In fact, it was not easy giving details to the reforms because the rot had been too comprehensive. The Bersih movement, supported by all the badly battered Opposition parties when it was founded in 2005, whose goal is to reform the electoral system, is in fact the most successful attempt at elucidating where the reversal of Malaysia's sad fortunes can begin. Attempts to corral high-level corruption as the cause of most ills in Malaysia have been plentiful as well, as has the highlighting of human rights violations. The revolt by the hard-pressed Indian community in the form of the Hindraf movement in late 2007 was a very significant one, even if it did not have the staying power that other movements, notably Bersih.

It is as if a new Malaysia, like a flying insect is waiting to be born, but its chrysalis has somehow grown leathery and will not give way. To cast off that now-unwelcomed sheath, critical help is apparently needed from unexpected actors. In this case, it is in the shape of Mahathir, who through an astounding display of strategic cunning accumulated over 70 years of involvement in politics managed to convince an Opposition that was partly welcoming of this intrusion and partly definitely not amused by it, that they needed him as much as he needed them.

The return of Mahathir will in time go down in Malaysian history as a narrative equal in virtuosity on the part of the 92-year-old embattled leader to any ancient Chinese story of unfathomable strategic brilliance. Now chairman of the Opposition coalition, Pakatan Harapan (PH), Mahathir is in the painful position of having to reboot the political system that he had played a central part in creating all his life. But then, to be fair, politics is about exercising effective manoeuvres within the immediate configuration of powerful forces as one understands them.

How Mahathir understands these forces today is something any scholar of Malaysian politics should not ignore. When the signified has run away from the signifier, when reality has changed beyond recognition, it would be foolish – or disingenuous, for anyone to insist that all is well.

While focusing on the aged Mahathir's return to politics – and on the Opposition side at that, and with many thinking that his new role perhaps suits him better than most of the others that he had had throughout his life, we should not forget the central role played by the young. It is in fact the Malaysians who were born during the Mahathir years who are the operative new factor in the political equation. That has been obvious ever since Mahathir sacked his deputy, Datuk Seri Anwar Ibrahim in 1998. Anwar refused to go quietly and in the process he emboldened a generation that transcended racial and religious divides to rise up against his enemy, Mahathir himself, who quickly came to symbolise all that was wrong with the system.

When Mahathir left the scene in late 2003, Malaysians thought that a page had been turned in their political history and they gave enormous support to his successor, Abdullah, for any reform he cared to mention. But Abdullah was not UMNO or BN, and the internal coherence of the party would not allow for reforms to get out of hand. And so, disappointed, many turned against him in 2008. His bad showing in the elections that year provided Najib with the chance to capture the UMNO presidency ironically supported by Mahathir from behind.

Najib had in fact been denied the post of deputy prime minister after the 1999 elections, but by 2008, Mahathir felt he had no other choice. By 2016, he became fully convinced that while Abdullah was ineffectual and open to manipulation by those close to him, Najib is much worse. For Mahathir now, Najib is a disaster.

And so, Mahathir, aged though he is, embarked on a pilgrimage to make one final attempt to reverse the direction of Malaysian politics. This time around, though, he has had to admit to himself that the forces that can help him are those arrayed against UMNO and BN. These are in fact the social and political forces mobilised by the detrimental effects of his king-making manoeuvrings in 1997–98 and in 2008–2009.

Disruptions to the Political Industry

Much blame for the ills that Malaysia now suffer can of course be put on the excess of identity politics that BN has relied on since its founding in the early 1970s to stay in power. But then, one does have to explain why this proven formula is failing now. The standard of governance has definitely been dropping drastically since 2009, which tells us that UMNO has lost the plot. Power had gone to its head more than ever before. But that is only one side of the story.

Another is how Malaysian society itself has changed. Global and regional power shifts, increased mobility and exposure, and social media and urbanisation have fashioned new mindsets that are not easily susceptible to twentieth-century methods of control. In fact, they may be averse to them. In saying this, I am also saying that Malaysia now exists in a global environment that is also greatly changed and that Malaysia's old-fashioned style of leadership cannot survive without undergoing a revolution of its own.

This new digital technology-driven environment, unlike any before, is relentless and dynamic. There is no dictator who decides its pace or its direction; it has a life of its own and it reduces all countries into mere respondents. This is why the term Industrialisation 4.0 has had to be coined – to explain this and to draw attention to its astounding impact. We are talking about a cultural revolution approaching on a global scale more than an industrial one.

Latecomers like China – once a communist regime, no less – have been able to respond well to the changes. For Malaysia, which is not a very late latecomer, to stumble, is understandable. But for it to stay down is not acceptable.

Now, in the twenty-first century, the link of political sentiments to technological innovations may not be easily observed but the indirect and deeper effects of the digital revolution and of the tsunami of social media in the last 20 years on human behaviour are certainly in plain sight. Most succinctly, the digital revolution has begun erasing the difference between rural and urban life. It has also made national boundaries more porous than ever. If properly governed, a country does not have to be a victim of this revolution. It should aim to ride the wave to its advantage instead.

Controlling the minds of citizens the twentieth-century way as a prerequisite for nation building will not work this century. In fact, in sad cases where governments continue to insist on it; it is at the cost of the country's economic development.

Disruptions to the political industry are happening all across the world in the best of countries and Malaysia is of course not immune to this process. Can the Malaysian butterfly break free of its calcified chrysalis and recreate the days when it was an Asian flying goose by accepting the challenges of the digital revolution, which it was already preparing for when Mahathir started the Multimedia Super Corridor in February 1996?

In fact, the problems that Vision 2020 and Bangsa Malaysia were supposed to be the answer to are still relevant today. Over the 20 years that the New Economic Policy (NEP) was officially in force, the concept of Malay special position transformed into the uncompromising idea of Ketuanan Melayu (Malay dominance), and inter-racial tensions evolved and intensified into inter-faith rows.

Mahathir's Vision 2020, which he proclaimed in 1991, was a recipe written to slow these trends and then to push the national agenda towards a more economic and culturally evolving consciousness. Buoyed by unprecedented economic growth in the 1990s, Mahathir's reputation as a champion of the Third World and leader of one of the amazing Asian flying geese was at its best. Malaysia's international stature was also at its peak.

But all that came to an end in September 1998. The Asian Financial Crisis began hitting the country and the region in mid-1997 in its political and economic belly and some would argue that the country is still unable to straighten itself up yet, 20 years later. Needless to say, the country's international reputation has perhaps dropped to its lowest since independence.

Although it was in 1998 that the call for reform was raised most loudly, and against Mahathir, Vision 2020 itself was a revolutionary idea boldly propounded as a challenge to hardcore Malay nationalists.

Anwar managed to front the broad dissent against Mahathir and BN, and integrate its different segments into a coalition movement that although it went through several difficult phases, survived as PH.

Looking back over the last two decades, one must say that the period marked by Anwar Ibrahim's refusal to disappear from the Malaysian scene in 1998 did ignite a sense of political agency and urgency in a whole generation of Malaysians. That is a trend that is hard to ignore. We saw a large segment of the Malay community demanding change in 1999, but which paradoxically pushed the non-Malays to stay with BN for fear of the unknown and of PAS' Islamist agenda.

Elections in 2004 saw a coming together of the electorate to give Abdullah a chance, while 2008 and 2013 can be seen as successive expressions of disappointment with UMNO's ability to reform itself. Now, as the fourteenth general election draws near, one could argue that Anwar's contradistinctive stance to BN and UMNO as corrupt, riddled with cronyism and authoritarian over the last 20 years could only take the movement to a certain extent. And that extent was reached in 2013 –an argument enhanced by the fact that break-ups began soon after within Pakatan Rakyat.

Mahathir lived long enough to see how the centralised apparatus he created for his own ends could be easily corrupted to serve the narrow interests of leaders much less concerned about nation-building than he was. To return to the fray in a convincing fashion, he had to have a political army behind him, and despite all the odds, he managed to convince members of Anwar's coalition that his new Parti Pribumi Bersatu Malaysia could deliver the crucial Malay support the coalition needs if it is to topple the BN government.

And so, over the last 30 years, what we have seen is how the rhetoric of NEP/Ketuanan Melayu was overshadowed for a while by Vision 2020/Bangsa Malaysia, which in turn was overwhelmed by the Reformasi Movement of 1998. Then came Abdullah's reform agenda in 2004, which was altered by Najib into a transformation agenda in 2009.

Given this backdrop, what the Opposition under Mahathir now tries to postulate for Malaysia's future can be seen as an unexpected though rational merging of the Reformasi Movement with the Vision 2020 agenda. What may work against them is the fact that the lengthy transition has brought political fatigue to some voters and this can weaken the Opposition come voting day.

For the Opposition, getting people out to vote and getting overseas Malaysians to care enough about home to return to hand in their ballots will be the key tactical concern.

To end on a speculative note, there are certain scenarios that are worth considering as Malaysia heads into what appears to be its most crucial election:

- A loss for PH will spell difficult times for Mahathir's new party and for Amanah. Their ability to survive will be severely tested.

- A victory for BN may see a strengthened PAS push its Islamist agenda across the country unless its association with UMNO sees its followers deserting it in large enough numbers.

- A BN euphoric over a big victory may see it move to crush – through institutional, legal and other means – any substantive Opposition left standing.

- Federal relations with the states won by PH will worsen further.

- East Malaysia's king-maker role will continue no matter what the results are nationally.

- Where international relations are concerned, not much change is to be expected.

Beyond

9 MAY
2018

47

The Bewildering Game of Malaysian Politics, the Rot Within the Barisan Nasional*

And so it has finally happened. Malaysia's Barisan Nasional (BN), who lost the majority vote but won the elections in 2013, now loses the power it had held since independence.

How could it fail so badly? It had the powers of incumbency with which it could move the goalposts whenever it needed to.

It had the means and a record of buying up the referee, the players and the linesmen. And it had endless yellow and red cards that it happily used to send its opponents off the field.

Seriously, it effectively owned the stadium along with the sports channels covering the game as well.

So wherein lay its weaknesses in the general elections of 2018?

The biggest flaw, most analysts would agree, was its president, Prime Minister Najib Razak, the leader of UMNO, which is the heart and soul of the coalition.

Tainted by suspicions of wrongdoing since long before he became Prime Minister following a coup against Abdullah Badawi in 2009, his term in office continued to be plagued by serious scandals such the murder of Mongolian model Altantuya Shaariibuu and the 1MDB

---

* *ChannelNewsAsia*, Commentaries, 10 May 2018.

affair which was investigated by a list of countries, including the US, Switzerland and Singapore.

When Najib saw in the results of the 2013 elections that he could not win back the Chinese Malaysian community, he appeared to give up on the middle ground – something that is rather irrational in a multiracial country like Malaysia – and began courting the more extreme elements among Malay nationalists and Islamists.

This modus operandi seemed to work though, and it led to the Pakatan Rakyat breaking up.

In Full Battle Gear, Mahathir Emerges

However, in this endless process of political manipulations, he brought a new player into the game against him – the retired long-term Prime Minister Mahathir Mohamad. At which point exactly Mahathir ushered himself back into the game is no longer really important.

What is important is that Mahathir, though 92 years of age, came out in full battle gear, swearing to dislodge Najib and to bring him to justice for his alleged abuse of power and corruption, and perhaps most poignantly, for his alleged disregard of UMNO's responsibility to build the nation.

Now, in the bewildering game that is Malaysian politics, Mahathir is historically and unquestionably the most effective striker ever. He never plays to lose. He is quite clearly the Pele of Malaysian politics, bar none.

In the penalty shootout that the election campaign of 2018 actually was, the BN side seemed to miss most of its shots.

Najib's decision to choose Wednesday as the polling day and yet not immediately declare it a national holiday, to have the shortest campaign period legally allowed and to ban Mahathir's new party from political activities just before he announced polling day, brought, among many other miscalculations, a backlash that in the end strengthened the Malay tsunami that had been predicted by Pakatan Harapan strategist Liew Chin Tong.

Pakatan Harapan did not miss many shots at goal, and when the last penalty kick had been taken, it had won 122 of the 222 parliamentary seats available according to reports, 11 more than it needed to win the match.

Who to Blame?

With hindsight, one should also ask what BN could have done differently?

Many would agree that once the 1MDB case was covered up time and time again, more and more steam built up within UMNO itself, leading in the end to fatal splits that finally moved the Malay electorate to vote for former UMNO leaders rather than present ones.

Had UMNO changed its president a year or so before the elections were called, and more credible and trusted leaders put in place instead and all that done before Mahathir felt compelled to take the field, all of BN's political advantages would have worked in its favour and the opposition parties relegated by the breakdown of Pakatan Rakyat, would never have been able to bully the sitting government.

But to put all the blame on Najib would not be correct either.

Much blame should also be put on the evolution of UMNO and of BN into a state where a leader like Najib could act with such impudence as he did when caught in the 1MDB and other scandals, where all internal dissent had been nullified and where all external opposition was rendered unthreatening.

Strange Bedfellows

There is of course also that important factor of the Reformasi Movement. Malaysia had been in transition away from Mahathirism, i.e. excessive authoritarianism since 1998.

But the two prime ministers who took over after Mahathir retired in 2003 – Abdullah Badawi and Najib – never lived up to expectations. The rot continued.

The amazing paradox was that Mahathir himself led the movement formed to fight him. Anwar Ibrahim's camp and Mahathir's camp became strange bedfellows when Najib's style of running the government stirred up such resentment in these two that Pakatan Harapan finally realised that Mahathir was the only one who could win the Malay vote they would need to take power.

In a strange twist of fate, the ambitions of the Reformasi Movement became fellow travellers with the man whose greatest success was his coinage of Vision 2020 and Bangsa Malaysia. He will now with all probability lead the country into that fateful year when Malaysia is meant to stand as a beacon of hope for the region and the developing world.

48

A Revolution in Malaysia?
Not so Fast...[*]

Now when it finally happens, it seems to have been inevitable all along and only a matter of time. But let's be honest. It certainly did not feel that way, not even when polling day began. For most Malaysians, toppling the Barisan Nasional (BN) was simply not possible.

BN had after all ruled Malaya/Malaysia since independence. It started out as the Alliance in its first nationwide elections in 1955, expanded to become BN for the 1974 elections and has remained the central power ever since.

And for a large part of that period, Mahathir Mohamad was its president.

It also had the undying loyalty of many in the Malay community, and could count on the over-represented East Malaysian states of Sabah and Sarawak to stay in power at the federal level.

What nobody on Earth could have imagined was that the finally successful attack on the BN would be led by Mahathir himself. In giving credit to him for this historically stunning achievement, one should not for a second diminish the resilience and courage of so many now grouped under the banner of the Pakatan Harapan that now takes on the exciting but daunting task of reforming Malaysia.

These people include most notably Lim Kit Siang, the supremo of the Democratic Action Party (DAP), the only major party that refused

---

[*] *South China Morning Post*, Hong Kong, 11 May 2018.

187

to join the BN in the early 1970s. This refusal saw it becoming more and more of a Chinese Malaysian-based organisation over time despite its official ideology of being multicultural. This was a condition that was effectively used against it by BN leaders and a fate that hung like an anchor around its neck for more than four decades. But it survived and could, when the time was ripe, help form the new coalition that now sends BN packing. Lim's political fervour obviously inspired his son, Lim Guan Eng, who was jailed twice by the BN regime but who against all odds, became the frontman for DAP and the chief minister of the rebel state of Penang since 2008.

Then there is Anwar Ibrahim of course, the deputy prime minister sacked and persecuted in 1997–98 by then-prime minister Mahathir. His continued struggle to topple the BN saw him jailed again, and now he watches his coalition triumph from within prison walls. Using the rallying cry of 'Reformasi', he galvanised a generation of young Malaysians who were too idealistic to deem it impossible to topple the BN and all that it had come to stand for – racialism, corruption, arrogance and generally bad, short-sighted policymaking.

Over the many years during which he suffered persecution, his wife, Wan Azizah Wan Ismail and his daughters, such as the eldest Nurul Izzah, suffered in desperation along with him and fought the political battle for him alongside his many followers, such as Mat Sabu and many others. They formed Parti Keadilan Rakyat, fronted by the watchful-eye banner that so faithfully represented Pakatan Harapan at the 2018 polls.

The brave generation that came of age when the Reformasi movement was in full swing provided the persistent support that helped Pakatan Harapan reach its major goal – becoming the government of Malaysia.

A page turns and BN as it has existed for so many decades is in deep crisis. Without the power of patronage that was its lifeblood, it is unlikely that it will remain in its present form. Splits should be expected, especially when member parties such as the Malaysian Chinese Association, the Malaysian Indian Congress and Parti Gerakan Rakyat have all been practically wiped out. The United Malays National Organisation (UMNO), though still a formidable party, cannot but go through a period of serious soul-searching during which many younger leaders will seize the chance to push aside the older generation that they must now blame for the party's debacle.

The BN's greatest challenge now is to study the Malaysian political landscape as if it were an alien planet. After all, the electoral results do show it to be badly out of sync with popular sentiments. It will have to seek new relevance and go beyond despair, defensiveness and resentment. Intuitively, making things difficult for the new government will be the most attractive path for it to take. After all, it has no experience with, nor will it have the right attitude for, opposition work. That is unfortunate but unavoidable to a large extent.

As a new day dawns in Malaysia, much of the planning, rebuilding and reforming by the new government will rely on Mahathir. In deference to his age and his experience, his coalition partners will watch and learn. At 92 years old, he may be the oldest newly elected leader in the world ever but his understanding of Malaysian governance is unmatched. In fact he is to blame for the compromised machinery of state that his erstwhile protégé Najib Razak took full advantage of. His promise now is to correct his past mistakes and to put Malaysian nation-building onto a new and more promising track.

The rise of China, India and other Association of Southeast Asian Nations offers no more time for mistakes and introverted governance.

Brought to power this second time around by a coalition created in painful opposition to an UMNO and BN that he had fostered, Mahathir will be closely watched by all for any signs of a return to authoritarian ways. His age makes such behaviour unlikely, however, as does the fact that he now so strangely symbolises reform and runs a government with Anwar's wife as deputy and Anwar supporters as members of his Cabinet.

A reform movement is not a revolution, and one should not expect the Pakatan Harapan government to reboot the whole nature of governance and political consciousness in the country. A country is not really something one can reboot. Instead, awaits is a process that sees changes sometimes coming in a rush, as should be the case in the first few months Pakatan Harapan is in power and sometimes perhaps imperceptibly. It will undoubtedly be a hopeful and exasperating process.

But it is a democratic movement, and it will therefore follow a trajectory drawn by contests and compromises between parties, coalitions and most notably between the government and the governed. The world will be watching, and a lot of hope will be placed on Malaysia by other societies in the region that still believe that democracy can actually bring personal freedom and national fulfilment.

49

Mahathir: Renaissance Man[*]

The word 'karma' is on the lips of Malaysians, at least of those who have some idea what the Sanskrit term means and who need to explain to themselves what has just taken place in their country.

The use of that resonant word is best understood through observation of the recent fates of Mahathir Mohamad and Anwar Ibrahim – the once almighty prime minister and icon of the Third World and his deputy whom he cruelly dismissed and jailed. Two men whose fates are connected the way that few are.

When the 92-year-old Mahathir, the past and present prime minister of Malaysia, decided to return to politics ostensibly to correct the mistakes he had made during his 22 years as leader of the country (1981–2003), onlookers nodded knowingly. The man had had the fortune to live long enough to baulk at the enduring effects of his wrongs. Whether that was good or bad fortune depended on what he intended to do about it.

'Karma's a bitch' was a casual but cutting phrase going around, one that summed up nicely Mahathir's ethical dilemma. On 5 September 2016 he had unexpectedly appeared as a member of the viewing public at a court hearing to greet Anwar. It was the first such encounter since the latter's sacking and subsequent jailing in 1998. That was Mahathir's first move at reconciliation with his protégé-turned-foe.

Mahathir was putting into play his plan to return to politics, 13 years after his retirement, in order to topple the prime minister, Najib Razak. And the opposition fronted by Anwar, once formed to oppose

---

* *The Tea House*, published by *Mekong Review*, 15 May 2018.

Mahathir himself, was the only force nearly capable enough of pulling off that stunt. What that opposition effectively lacked was strong enough support from the Malay community outside of the urban areas. This Mahathir could provide.

Since his retirement in October 2003, Mahathir had been watching and meddling in the politics of his successors. He appeared to evince greater and greater despair at what he had done during his tenure when his authoritarian methods undid many of the checks and balances that had been Malaysia's proud though slowly eroding legacy.

A total of 18 years of hurt and pain separated Mahathir and Anwar when they met in court that day. These two men were once the 'dream team' government – when the country enjoyed the status of being one of Asia's golden geese of economic growth and a beacon for developing nations. Anwar's *Asian Renaissance* was published in 1996 to herald the approaching age of Asian economic prowess and moral leadership. That was two years before he was jailed for abuse of power and sodomy, charges always properly seen to be politically motivated.

While neighbouring countries such as Indonesia and Thailand saw their regimes fall in the wake of the Asian financial crisis that began in 1997, Malaysia continued chugging along; its crippled political establishment saved by Mahathir's insistence on pushing ahead without external help and without institutional reforms, and with its economy falling into deeper and deeper debt. His then nemesis, Anwar, though in prison, came to represent the call for change. And his supporters rallied under the cry of 'Reformasi'.

Despite strong showings by the opposition in the elections of 2008 and 2013, the fortress that is the Barisan Nasional (National Front) coalition led by the United Malays National Organisation (which had ruled the country continuously since independence in 1957) withstood the onslaught of discontent. For good measure, Najib put Anwar back in jail in 2014.

For two decades, then, Malaysia endured an era of suspended transition that threatened to become the new normal – at least until 9 May 2018.

Mahathir formed a new party and managed to convince Anwar's supporters in the Pakatan Harapan coalition not only to embrace it but also to make him the coalition's chairman. The opposition parties knew all too well that it was heading for another failure in the coming elections and that Mahathir was their only hope. And so Pakatan Harapan went into battle led by Mahathir, their former arch-enemy, with Anwar's wife, Wan Azizah Wan Ismail, as his deputy and all under the banner of Anwar's party, Parti Keadilan Rakyat (People's Justice Party).

The shocking election results that came in through the night on Wednesday could not have been predicted except by those who were merely going for the highest possible odds given by bookies. The once all-powerful Barisan Nasional lost power in all but three of the country's 13 states.

The joining of forces by Mahathir and Anwar had proven successful and decisively so. Not one to hesitate, especially now when he has much to do and little time in which to do it, Mahathir acted quickly on his promise to get a pardon for Anwar. And so less than a week after he returned as prime minister, Mahathir righted one of the cruellest and significant wrongs that stained his earlier tenure. Anwar will be released to the fresh air of a new Malaysia.

Mahathir was given the chance to free the man he had once jailed. He now also has the chance to reform Malaysia's governance and as he has promised, hand over power to Anwar within two years.

Not many are given that blessing to correct grave wrongs within one lifetime. A karmic circle has been allowed to close. For the country, the lessons learned from the Asian financial crisis may now be put to good use, and this will have positive repercussions for the rest of the region, if not the world.

50

Malaysia's Reformasi Movement Lives Up to Its Name*

A Silent and Peaceful Revolution

A revolution took place in Malaysia on 9 May 2018. It was a silent and peaceful one, amazingly achieved through the ballot box and is therefore not noticed for what it is. But it is a revolution nevertheless and the effects of it are moving like a strong undercurrent throughout the nation – cutting down old structures, be these mental ones, social ones or political ones. A sense of jubilation and disorientation now permeates the country and will do so for a few weeks yet, if not months.

For people in the states of Penang and Selangor, which had been governed by federal opposition parties for the last ten years, the sudden change whereby the federal power is now an intimately friendly one is dizzily baffling. From being necessarily defensive, strategic and reactive in all they did to parry an antagonistic central power, they now have the weird opportunity to dream big. It will take a while before they can do that with gusto and confidence. Their old habits will die hard. Some hesitation is to be expected, along with much resentment against those who had supported the fallen government so unconscionably. Some frames of thought will appear clearly outdated, and when expressed will sound revisionist or obsolete.

Economically, there is good reason to hope that the country can now live up to its potential again, that many of its migrated sons and

---

* *Heinrich Boll Stiftung* (South East Asia), Commentaries, 15 May 2018.

daughters, now well trained in foreign lands, will return to help put the country back on track and that the recent fall of the ringgit will be reversed.

This toppling of a regime that had been in place since independence in 1957 occurs two decades after the country lost its ability in 1997–98 to soar with fellow Asian flying geese. And with the change in government, it is now finally able to put the lessons it learned – or should have learned – from the Asian Financial Crisis to good use.

While countries such as South Korea, Thailand and Indonesia experienced immediate regime change and institutional reforms that today have left them as unrecognisably different entities from what they were in the Roaring 90s, Malaysia came through that period with its political system intact. That was partly due to the doggedness of then-prime minister Mahathir Mohamad in rejecting external assistance and interference.

But for that achievement, the country had to pay a price. It suffered greater inter-ethnic divisiveness, plunging competence in governance, stupefying levels of corruption and worst of all, a huge loss of public faith in its ability to ever become a developed nation. The notions of 'Bangsa Malaysia' (Malaysian Nation) and 'Vision 2020', pushed strategically into public discourse in the early 1990s by Mahathir to engender a stronger sense economic nationalism among his countrymen, also went down in the Crisis.

The 20-year-old Reformasi Movement

Along with it fell Anwar Ibrahim, Mahathir's deputy prime minister and finance minister. Apparently, in being too keen on IMF intrusion into the Malaysian political economy, he brought the wrath of his boss, Mahathir, upon himself. Sacked and subsequently jailed for 12 years in 1999 for abuse of power and for sodomy, Anwar's downfall gave birth to a reform movement that would not be denied. Indeed, a whole new generation of young Malaysians, generally well educated, well informed and deeply urban, was inspired by the open battle between the two political giants, who soon turned protesting and demonstrating on the streets into a habit and an art of war.

Their general call for comprehensive reforms quickly defined public discourses and convinced even the establishment to the extent that under Mahathir's successor Abdullah Badawi in 2003, the government adopted 'reforms' as its biggest promise to the electorate. True to that spirit, Abdullah did not stand in the way of the appeals court when it decided in favour of Anwar on a technicality and released the prisoner after he had served six years of his two six-year consecutive sentences.

But in the end, Abdullah's reform agenda was seen by many to be a failure. In the meantime, the opposition had, together with many non-government organisations, formed a body to call for electoral reforms. It went under the name The Coalition for Clean and Fair Elections (Bersih, Malay for 'clean') and through a hugely successful street demonstration in Kuala Lumpur in November 2007, it inspired a strong swing in public sentiments against the federal government. The issue of elections is of course one that is not communal or racial in character and it allowed for a coming together of activists of all communities. This 40,000-strong rally was followed in December that year by another unexpectedly large demonstration, this one led by the Hindu Rights Action Force (Hindraf).

Quite unaccountably, in the face of these strong anti-government sentiments, Abdullah ill-advisedly called for early elections in March 2008. Riding on the tide of discontent, the opposition parties managed to agree on a concerted electoral strategy under the leadership of Anwar Ibrahim. This move proved successful and together, they won power in five of Malaysia's 13 states. They also denied the ruling coalition the supermajority in parliament that it had always enjoyed. Constitutional amendments in Malaysia require support from two-thirds of parliamentarians to pass.

Stunned by this loss in seats, in power and in face, the United Malays National Organisation (UMNO) ousted Abdullah as its president a year into his second term as prime minister. This move was and is widely understood to have been orchestrated by Mahathir from within. Najib Razak now became UMNO's president, and by virtue of that, also the country's prime minister. This was a role that he apparently considered a birthright, given that his father, Abdul Razak Hussein, was prime minister from 1970 to 1976 and is still honoured by the Malay community today as 'Bapa Pembangunan' (Father of

Development). Razak was also the man who brought Mahathir back in from the cold in 1973, four years after he was expelled from the party for calling for the resignation of the first prime minister, Tunku Abdul Rahman Putra.

Najib, rightly reading the spirit of the times, assumed the word 'transformation' to describe his key policies, in acceptance of the fact that the public still considered reforms a primary goal in the post-Mahathir era. His administration also coined 'One Malaysia' in imitation of Mahathir's 'Bangsa Malaysia'. The target for the country to reach developed nation status by the year 2020 was kept unchanged despite the fact that the economic and statistical trajectories by then all showed that ambition to be an impossibility.

When his attempt at winning back the electoral middle ground – meaning the urban population, especially the Chinese vote – failed, as became obvious in the 2013 general elections during which his ruling coalition lost the popular vote for the first time in its history, he swung to the right. This he did in two related arcs. While pandering to Malay extremists, he at the same time encouraged or at least avoided discouraging expressions of Muslim fundamentalism in the multicultural country.

This proved strategically effective in that Najib was soon able to draw PAS, the Islamist party that was a member of the opposition coalition, to push for Islamist legislation in parliament. Such a move could only end in a break-up of that coalition since the DAP, the Chinese-based multiracial and nominally social democratic party, was expected to and did oppose it vehemently.

This may have weakened the opposition considerably but it did not win the BN much extra support. In fact, it can be compellingly argued that Najib's cosying up to extremists accelerated divisions among UMNO supporters –with decisively detrimental results for the party come election time in 2018.

Horrified at the bigotry of the extremists, some in the Malay community, both young and old, began slowly but steadily to speak out against the regime. In the meantime, Najib had Anwar jailed on a charge of sodomy when the latter tried by way of a by-election to become the chief minister of the rich state of Selangor.

What made things increasingly intolerable for many Malaysians were the scandals that seemed to circle the Prime Minister. These included suspicions of a shady submarine deal done between Malaysia and France when Najib was minister of defence, which had been hanging over him for years and of course the murder of Altantuya Shaariibuu, a female Mongolian national who had played an assortment of roles in the arms deal. Her body was blown up with military grade explosives outside Kuala Lumpur. Two bodyguards assigned to the Najib household were found guilty of this crime although the motive was never ascertained. Several strange murders, disappearances and deaths occurred over the few years that Najib was in power.

And then the 1MDB scandal broke. The intricacies of this phenomenon are too many to describe here but suffice it to say that Najib, soon after taking power in 2009 had started a sovereign investment fund called 1MDB through which he is now being investigated for using to finance his political machinery and from which billions are purported to have been channelled overseas for the enjoyment of individuals close to his family. The case has allowed foreign powers to brand Malaysia a kleptocracy and several countries including the USA, Singapore and Switzerland have been investigating cash transfers and money laundering related to 1MDB. Indeed, it is generally suspected that it was this scandal that brought Mahathir back into politics to unseat Najib.

If that was the case, it could then also be the case that gave Mahathir the epiphany that his style of running the government all those years ago was now bringing ruin to the country. He could now not die without righting those wrongs. Now that he has done more than anyone could ask for by way of repentance, he will go down in the history books as the man who had made it possible for others to almost destroy the country but who at great cost returned to right this wrongs to the extent it was possible to right them. The picture of Mahathir greeting Anwar on the latter's release on 16 May 2018 is therefore a poignant moment that was in effect the closing of a karmic circle.

The Future is Now

The electoral victory of the Pakatan Harapan was indeed a convincing one. It leaves the Barisan Nasional governing only three states – tiny

Perlis at the Thai border, Najib's home state of Pahang and the giant state of Sarawak. Had the margin been small, the change in power might not have happened given the Barisan's history of electoral trickery.

What seems clear at this point is that UMNO and BN are paying the ultimate price for refusing to carry out reforms when they had the chance. The BN will now almost definitely disappear. Apart from UMNO, its members on the peninsula are as good as wiped out, its members in Sabah are leaving in a rush and signs are pointing to a strong possibility that BN parties in Sarawak will also leave but without joining Pakatan. No doubt UMNO still has 54 seats in parliament but it is a party in decline and support for it is bound to drop much further before it has any chance of rebounding.

The Reformasi era in Malaysia – at least its initial stage – is therefore bookended by the street demonstrations of September 1998 at one end and by its political manifestation, the Pakatan Harapan coalition, taking power in May 2018 at the other end. More poignantly, it is framed by the jailing of Anwar Ibrahim by Prime Minister Mahathir Mohamad in 1998 to his release in 2018 by the past and present Prime Minister Mahathir Mohamad.

During its first ten days in power, the Pakatan Harapan government led by Mahathir Mohamad had already fulfilled more of the promises made during the election campaign than anyone could have imagined possible. Among some other awe-inspiring things, Mahathir freed Anwar Ibrahim, stopped Najib and his wife from leaving the country and initiated an investigation against the fallen prime minister. He cut the hugely unpopular goods and services tax (GST) down to zero per cent, and in a move that pleases the Chinese Malaysian population and the stock market greatly, made DAP secretary-general Lim Guan Eng the finance minister of the country. Lim Guan Eng was the chief minister of the rebel state of Penang in the last ten years who had managed its economy well and put certain transparent policies into place.

Creating a cabinet that is acceptable to all the parties in the victorious Pakatan Harapan is no easy task, and early delays caused some worry among observers.

The education system in Malaysia has been deteriorated in recent decades, and many therefore thought it was a wise move when he took on the additional portfolio as Minister of Education. However, the public quickly reminded him that his manifesto did promise that no prime minister is ever to hold a second portfolio at the same time, especially the finance portfolio. He quickly backed down and appointed the lecturer Maszlee Malik to that position instead.

The sense of hope is strong in Malaysia at the moment, as is the sense of bewilderment and disorientation. But there is also a strong sense of empowerment and of a growing willingness to forgive the past sins and past cowardice of fellow Malaysians.

The future has arrived for the Reformasi Movement and for Malaysia. Now in power, there is much reforming of the system to get on with.

51

In Lieu of Race and Religion...*

One can easily see how southern Southeast Asia, being largely maritime, ethnically very diverse and historically and geo-economically a collection of trade routes, in dividing itself into zealous and jealous nation-states over the last century, would as a region see prescribe racial and religious sentiments in the creating of stable national, ethnic majorities.

To be sure, the creation of a politically relevant sense of ethnic commonality has almost always depended on a synchronised proselytisation of a common religion. Thus, communal sentiments have more often than not been constructed by means of an emotive complex of religious control and race construction.

This begs the question, how then is peaceful multicultural life even possible? And relatedly, why would a project of ethnic identity even allow itself to be open-ended and contaminated? Let me in a hasty fashion list some points that I think can help the discussion along.

1. The Contingency of Ethnic Identity Creation

To start with, ethnicities are not as stable units of identity and community as one might think. Indeed, the project of ethnicity creation is in itself a deceptive undertaking. I would claim it to be a political game played in the interest of a select group more than it is a description of unchanging reality. In Karl Marx's exaggeration, it is necessarily a false identity.

---

* *The Edge*, Malaysia, 27 May–2 June 2018.

But what comes first? The need to survive or the need to identify? Now, I can agree that since a group is stronger than an individual, group identification immediately increases the chances of survival enormously. Beyond a certain level though, the economic gains to be had from inter-ethnic collaboration becomes obvious. Close societies seem therefore to be rather unstable. One of the greatest political paradoxes in human history is that empires tend necessarily towards multiculturalism while nation-states move in the opposite direction and exert petty control over the expressions of identity of its citizens.

2. **International Economic Mutualism**

What humanity has learned more clearly than ever now is that economic interaction between nations and polities is done because it is mutually beneficial. In fact, the post-World War II, post-colonial, post-Cold War era is a period where economic interaction and the conditions needed to sustain and develop international trade are recognised and pursued as the remedy for international war. The main lesson learned from the wars of the last century then is that economic mutualism is the best means for tempering the ethnocentric tendencies of nations.

With economic mutualism amongst nations and the social constructs that grow out of it, ethnic identities become fluid and less emotive.

This seems a safe and sound solution except for one simple dynamic – the tendency for economic gaps, be these income-based, educational, developmental, digital, etc., to grow exponentially.

3. **Gaps in the System**

Also, at a certain stage, the threat to emotive identity, often coupled with one or another of these gaps initiates a backlash and an understandable burst of defensive nationalism. To an extent, that was what happened in 2016 with the election of the Donald Trump presidency and the Brexit vote in the United Kingdom.

Significantly, the margins of victory were small in both cases, and one should not exaggerate the intensity of the nationalist pathos involved in the backlash. No doubt, local values and conditions are challenged or destroyed by free trade, but much of the anger is probably due to the growing income and developmental gap between regions in the same nation-state and the lack of positive government measures to offset the long-term detrimental effects of free trade.

Finally, let me comment within this context on the silent revolution that the result of the recent Malaysian general elections amounts to.

Hardly anywhere else in the world had arguments in a democracy been so openly and unabashedly based on (religion-defined) as in Malaysia. And when the political parties that had been ruling the country for over 60 years finally fell on 9 May, the heavy task placed on the new government is that of stopping a return to politicking based on race and religion.

Awareness of Class, Society and the World

To apply the three points made earlier, one can say that the race categories in Malaysia are hugely exaggerated, unscientific and piggybacked on the exigencies of the colonial masters and the Japanese invaders. Also, since Day One, Malaysia's economic structure has been an international one. Securing a place within the regime of international free trade, even if limited at times for various reasons, has therefore always been the raison d'etre for its foreign policies.

As the various gaps that have been mentioned grew, the old Malaysian government had failed to close them with proper sustainable policies of the social democratic kind to provide for the future and to develop the potential of young Malaysians. Instead, money politics became the order of the day. It failed to replace stop-gap methods with serious gap-closing measures.

Beyond these three points are three others that have special significance for Malaysia's ambition to rise beyond identity politics and which should be mentioned here.

First, grey areas in ethnic identity and cultural expressions need to be accepted as par for the course. If ethnic groups are hindered from broad interaction and from inter-marriage, then one cannot expect them to show encouraging signs of assimilation even in the long run. Nation building under such circumstances can only succeed to a limited extent. Natural cultural assimilation needs to be allowed, which also means that clear definitions of race and religion have to fade away.

Secondly, the best mindset change that I can imagine to be possible for Malaysia to move away from its fixation with race and religion is for its citizens to become sociologically conscious. Realising how sociological perspectives enhance empathy in society, deconstruct collective identities and dismantle ethnic prejudices will diminish the relevance and validity of race-based arguments. More clearly, class arguments can replace identity politics.

The third has to do with Malaysia's place in the region and the world. More focus on international affairs in the country's public discourses will help limit the fixation with its parochialism.

52

It All Seems So Simple Now...*

Into the great dining hall, the children came. The guards at the gates do their best to keep as many of them out as possible, but they are too few and the children have become many and they have become good at pushing their way in. They gather eagerly despite feeling unwelcomed because this hall is opened only once every five years for the grand dinner. And everyone can talk that day. Over time, the children have learned that if they are precise in their language, and if they speak in unison, their voices can actually echo nicely and fill the room.

They tend to assemble in several big groups. There are those who rush to come close to the head of the table where the food is served first and where the favours of the master of ceremony are dispensed most freely. Then there are those who sit slightly to the side, sulky but hopeful of some attention from the main table. At the far end of the room gather those who have given up on ever getting to the main table and they mix in uncomfortably with those furthest away who prefer the fresher air closest to the tall windows.

There are always some who prefer to hang around outside the swinging doors that lead into the kitchen, not caring that being close to where the food is being prepared does not mean that they get served first, or at all. But they are hopeful. And every now and then, one of them manages to sneak in to satiate themselves unnoticed.

It is otherwise all meant to be rather formal and ritualistic, like a sun-worshipping ceremony that starts with the sun rising and that ends

---

* Editorial, *Penang Monthly*, June 2018.

when the sun goes behind the first clouds, and whose real significance few remember any longer, least of all the masters of ceremony.

It is all often more reminiscent of mealtime at some Dickensian orphanage, where one gets one's share – and often less – and any request for more is rewarded with a sharp slap or with detention.

But this year, 2018, 9 May, the often oppressive and unhappy atmosphere in Malaysia Hall feels strangely different. Perhaps it is because the windows over time no longer shut very well and more fresh air than normal now fills the room. The children had always been told that too much fresh air is bad for them. Or it may be that more and more of the children have grown up and are talking less in a whisper than normal, as if they have forgotten that some guard may be among them, sinisterly hidden among them, out of uniform.

They do well to remember though, for some of them have been punished before, and a few just the day earlier. In fact, one of the elder ones is still locked away in the cellar with a bad back on long-term detention. On the last two occasions, this growing group sitting far from the main table had been a little too loud for the comfort of those at the main table and some of them had had to suffer the consequences. Less food than ever was passed down.

But perhaps the change in the atmosphere is because the children notice that the old and retired master of ceremony whose voice for many years once resonated so sharply and scarily within these walls demanding order is sitting with them by the windows and as far away from the main table as he can get. To everyone's surprise, he seems to agree with them that the arrangement of the furniture in Malaysia Hall needs to change so that more food can be brought in faster and served more quickly to all ends of the room.

And so, knowing better than anyone else what things look like from the main table, he is telling them to synchronise their voices better than ever and to shout down the groups gathered around the more succulent dishes.

They now know that if they do that well, those at the fringes will join in and together their voice will be strong and there may be enough of them to rearrange the furniture themselves in such a way that each will have a better chance of getting some good bits from the best dishes and so that the food can be passed around more happily and generously. And with everyone pushing, they may even be able to get the windows opened wide. More fresh air will be let in then to invigorate everyone.

Furthermore, the separate groups will no longer be able to sit so far away from each other.

The whole of Malaysia Hall can be transformed and the voices of even the littlest ones heard.

And so, with synchronised effort, they push the windows open, letting out stale air and letting the breeze and the cheers of the outside world in. And they begin rearranging the tables and chairs, singing as they do so. All that will take some time to get into place but it all seems so simple now...

Catharsis – The Rebirth of Malaysia Finally Begins*

Maybe it was because the transition took so long and opposition parties had had a chance to rule certain states for two terms and made a change in government an acceptable event. Maybe it was because the fear that Malaysians have a hidden tendency for violent rioting is simply a bad myth kept alive by the federal government that concentrated power unto itself following the 1969 racial killings. Maybe it was because Najib Razak's administration had brought profound shame unto his countrymen. Maybe Malaysians had matured on the sly more than even they themselves had realised. Or maybe it was because the battering ram that finally brought down the defences of the Barisan Nasional (BN), had Mahathir Mohamad, the man who led BN for 22 years, as its head.

Whatever it was, the fall of the longest-ruling regime in a democratic country in the world came amazingly peacefully. In its fourteenth general elections held on 9 May 2018, the Malaysian opposition coalition, Pakatan Harapan, managed to win 122 (55 per cent) of the country's 222 parliamentary seats. A system of government that had always been accused of being but a sham democracy at worst and a semi-democracy at best suddenly crumbled and the long-awaited change in government occurred as smoothly as in any mature democracy.

But we know nevertheless that a revolution has just taken place. All comfort zones are being swept away, barely noticed because it is

---

* Cover story, *Penang Monthly*, June 2018.

happening in slow motion. If in no other field, the year 2020 when Malaysia is supposed to become an advanced country, appears to have come early where democracy is concerned!

Pundits have often said of the general elections of 8 March 2008 that it was a lucky thing for the country that the BN did not lose power unexpectedly and overnight. Instead, it lost control over five states and the two-thirds parliamentary majority, and therefore no rioting took place because not all was lost to BN and regaining lost support was considered totally possible. After all, Malaysia's electoral results had almost always shown a pattern where one bad election for the BN was followed by a good one.

Without having to go back too far, we saw for example that the Mahathir Mohamad administration enjoyed strong support in 1995, fared badly in 1999, boasted a record-strong showing in 2004 under Abdullah Badawi, who then followed that up with a record-weak election in 2008. So, in 2013, Najib Razak had good reason to think that his sloganeering style of leadership, where terms such as One Malaysia (1Malaysia), Government Transformation Programme (GTP), Economic Transformation Programme (ETP) and the New Economic Model (NEM) were propounded as profound and comprehensive reform policies and proclaimed as successes before any beneficial effects were felt by the population at large, was enough for him to regain ground. The macroeconomic data were not too bad considering that the world was in a depression. And what's more, the electoral pattern was on his side.

He was wrong, of course. In 2013, the BN retreated further and even lost the popular vote on the peninsula.

Breaking the Race Champion Myth

It is hard to disprove the claim that a staggered process in changing the government at the federal level is better and safer than an immediate turning of the page. There is probably some truth in that but to push that argument now is to delve in counterfactual speculation. Suffice it to say that the claim is not without substance.

Behind that claim, though, lies the assumption that the loss of power by BN and UMNO is equal to a definitive and irreversible loss of control by the Malay community as a whole over its own fate. That, after all, had always been UMNO's proffered bugbear to its supporters. And for that myth to work, the Chinese Malaysians had always had to be made by UMNO to play the bogeyman.

Thus, because the opposition coalition in 2008 was led by Anwar Ibrahim, the Chinese bogeyman in the form of the DAP was all the more necessary as a spook and Anwar had to be painted a puppet for the Chinese. Hiding the fact that both coalitions were led by Malay leaders, and which appeared equally strong, was a requirement to keep the racial division and mutually fearful sentiments alive. The same was true in 2013 but somehow the Chinese bogeyman did not seem to work very well any longer and that year, Najib failed to regain any ground lost by Abdullah Badawi in 2008.

That did not stop UMNO from making the desperate and ridiculous claim in 2018 that Mahathir Mohamad, now the leader of the opposition Pakatan Harapan, is a Chinese stooge. That claim was too outrageous for most Malays to believe and that in itself reveals how racial politics based on polarising the Malays from the non-Malays simply does not work any longer.

And so, due to larger processes of change such as urbanisation, education, social media and globalisation, UMNO's racial dichotomisation began failing without its propagators realising that the Malay community had become too diverse to be united through simply instigating fear of the Chinese. But then, they were blinded by their own propaganda. Changing a formula that had been successful for so long and reforming a party that has race championing as its *raison d'être* away from its ideology, could not happen unless the danger was recognised to be life-threatening. Apparently, UMNO and BN were simply too confident of their ability to manipulate the electoral process to their advantage should their manipulation of the people through their control of the mass media, the police and the judiciary fail; serious reforms were never considered. Adopting terms of reform was thought to be enough, if used alongside draconian means of control.

There have been countless signs over recent months that Najib had seriously lost touch with the electoral ground, if not with reality. To be sure, on the side of BN supporters, this was painfully clear when one considers how UMNO's allies within the coalition seemed unable to re-strategise their position and very often appeared content to rely on Big Brother UMNO to pull them through. Within UMNO, sounds of protest against what they now saw as parasitic behaviour by MCA, Gerakan and MIC, most notably, were heard more and more often as the elections drew closer.

Such were the mindsets perpetuated in the government camp. It will take a while before they can accept the change in government and all it means for their way of life, their career path, their social status and their sense of self-worth, not to mention the self-pity and self-blame that they will indulge in for not seeing the change coming and for being so silly as to have landed on the wrong side of history, as it were.

The Future Has Arrived

One expects people in the opposition camps, i.e. in the Pakatan parties on the one hand and in PAS on the other, to be more prepared for the changes that they were fighting for. To be sure, while the fall of the BN government is not a trauma for Pakatan people the way it is for BN supporters, it does not mean that their comfort zones did not disappear as surely as they did for the latter. For PAS perhaps, the psychological challenges are limited.

Nevertheless, victory, especially after an extended struggle, can be quite a shock to the psyche. After exultation comes disorientation. The defensive attitudes, the tactical frame of mind and the critical stance of those who had been opposed to the BN government, which have all served them so well and allowed them to remain sane, are now losing relevance. Without the all-powerful BN to orientate around, a deep sense of bewilderment creeps upon them. Bittersweet would be an appropriate term for it, however glib that may sound. Change is here and it is in the individual psyche that the most work needs to be done.

Many are the planned but unfinished policies in the opposition states whose relevance are now called into question. They have to be revisited and reviewed. The rationale for them is in many cases no longer valid. Since the pond in which they developed is now an ocean, one has to wonder if their effects if they are implemented will be as intended originally. The same applies to each individual who has in their minds and daily actions resisted the effects, both insidious and obvious, of BN rule and of the opposition against it.

The future is not tomorrow. It has arrived. It is today. And that of course brings some anxiety. It also means that the time of mere criticising, however well justified, is now over. Many are the books commenting on the sorry state of Malaysian socio-politics and socio-economics, which will now seem hugely uninteresting. That is the price of victory.

One is reminded of soldiers returning from a war. Their work into which they literally invested their lives is now over. It does not matter if they are on the winning side or not; for most of them, their relevance, their significance and their position will now begin to fade away.

For people at large, who have not been especially interested in politics one way or the other, the fact that a new era has arrived cannot go unnoticed. It affects them deeply, too. Ignorance is bliss only when the status quo is stable. When a revolution happens, however peacefully, the one who knows how the breezes blow and how the ocean flows, will feel more empowered and in control of his fate.

To keep to the notion of revolution, one could say that revisionist tendencies in the aftermath of great change are found in the resistance put up intuitively by the collective psyche. If we are used to thinking in terms of racial collectives and hierarchies; if we are used to fighting an invincible political structure; if we have been able to think of the country only as a middling society that should be happy with whatever comes along that is not the worst thing imaginable; if we have accepted that fellow human beings, just like ourselves, will be the mediocre creatures we run into every day, easily bribed and easily ignored; then we can be sure that cynicism is our comfort food and our psychological haven.

Healing the Nation's Post-traumatic Stress Injury

What made the general elections of 2018 so special is that the toppling of the old regime was effectuated with such a large margin. The 'Malay tsunami' that was coined by DAP strategist Liew Chin Tong, and used more prescriptively than descriptively, did come to pass. The change in government, given the manifest trickery of the BN, would not have been brought to completion otherwise.

To clarify through exaggeration, we should perhaps consider the country to be suffering from transitory post-traumatic stress disorder

(PTSD). The point is not to blacken what is truly a rosy picture but to draw attention to the profundity of the systemic change and find words for the mixture of feelings that Malaysians now experience, so that each will know that he or she is not alone in feeling them and that these feelings are a necessary but passing phase for any society that dares to topple a suppressive government. Interesting, doctors now wish to rename the condition an injury rather than a disorder. That may be more appropriate – we all carry some injury from the state of conflict that had passed for nation-building in Malaysia all these years. The disorder is over; it is time to heal injuries.

The bewilderment now felt by Malaysians began before the election itself, among other things when Mahathir Mohamad chose to return to politics and team up with Anwar Ibrahim – in effect merging the social and economic aspirations of Vision 2020 with the demands for institutional change championed by the Reformasi Movement. In gaining a royal pardon for Anwar Ibrahim just a week after returning to power, and in naming Lim Guan Eng, the Chief Minister of Penang as his Finance Minister, Mahathir managed to convince all and sundry that he is in truth adopting the reform agenda. More than that, naming a Malaysian of Chinese origin as Finance Minister appears to hark back to the early 1970s when inter-racial tensions were institutionalised and perpetuated through the adoption of the New Economic Policy, the formation of the BN, the muffling of parliament and Malay monopoly over all key ministries and to be as much as an attempt at closure for the agonies of that early era.

If seen that way, Mahathir has gone one step further than what even Reformasi diehards imagine. Again, I take that to further signify that the revolution by ballot box that Malaysians accomplished on 9 May 2018 is a deeply psychological one as much as it is a political one. This is because the BN, model of power for six decades employed insidious and devious methods to prey on and play with the minds of Malaysian citizens. Through the threat of near arbitrary punishment, through the myth of uncompromising racial and religious lines, and through the corruption of values through an ideology of racial privilege, it stunted the mental growth of the country, which one would argue is both the basic reason for gaining independence and the proper definition of decolonisation.

Mahathir himself was party to those processes. His willingness to rectify matters now should inspire his fellow countrymen to some deep self-analysis and to be morally sincere and bold in action and to make the most of their newfound freedom.

That is why some now call 9 May 2018 the second Merdeka Day. It should also be a day when we remind ourselves that the mental liberation of Malaysia from colonialism and post-colonialism is a staggered and continual process. And that process cannot be painless and easy. It has to be as cathartic as the injury has been comprehensive.

54

A Malaysian Spring for Intelligentsia?*

I know Malaysia is a tropical country, but let's adopt a concept from temperate zones without having to be politically sensitive about it. We are in the midst of a potent Malaysian Spring, and the way things are looking, a proper summer is to be expected. And by the time winter comes along many months down the road, we will all be — or on the way to being — properly nourished, physically safe and pleasantly housed.

In my experience, spring signals the arrival of an overpowering sense of hope. In Sweden, they call it "vårkänsla" — the feel of spring during which the need for all living beings to create and procreate, and to rejoice, is in painful excess.

Spring always makes the self-piteousness of the winter seem pathetic and irrelevant. And yet, the negation of the reasons for dark depression does not mean that the reasons for hope will naturally bear fruit. Even if the proverbial spring is a gift, the approaching summer is not. Instead, the summer has to be actively embraced; it is a time that calls for action if promise is to be fulfilled.

Freeing the Malaysian tongue

One sad long-term effect of the excessive control of free speech in Malaysia over the last few decades is that the culture of discussion and debate that we once enjoyed has been stifled. A new era may

---

* Editorial, *Penang Monthly*, June 2018.

be beginning, but a new ethos of fearless yet responsible voicing of opinions will appear only if actively encouraged and cultivated, and by as many Malaysians as possible.

In an ideal country that is free and bold, public discourses would be stimulated by its universities and journalists. In the far-from-ideal country that Malaysia has been, where student life for decades was dissociated on pain of serious punishment from public expressions of interest in politics, the ability to engage in subtle and thoughtful discussions about such matters was naturally stunted. The Universities and University Colleges Act 1971 made sure of that.

For journalists, there exists a broader spectrum of legislation for their persecutors and prosecutors to choose from. If the Security Offences (Special Measures) Act 2012 that replaced the Internal Security Act 1960 did not suffice for some reason, then there was always the Sedition Act 1948. Furthermore, most newspapers are owned by political parties, which has acted as an effective muzzle on its once best and bravest news hounds.

No doubt, some concrete changes where freedom of speech is concerned will be taking place under the new government that took over in May.

But Malaysians must now learn to break the bad habits that decades of timid living under an authoritarian system has forced upon them. Aside from the need for journalism to recover its lost professionalism, passion and ideals, it must now compete with the loose-cannon quick-satisfaction style of writing that the blogging era has released upon society. Sensationalism was already a bane long before social media made it possible for every man, woman and child to express themselves without the inconvenience of filtering their words. The need to opine is now much stronger than the wish to carry on an intelligent conversation.

Much is also expected of new Minister of Education Maszlee Malik in his attempt to remodel the school system. He will need every ounce of his reformist passion to stay on course and achieve visible and tangible results in the next few years. He needs all the help he can get from the rest of us.

We are all journalists and debaters now.

But journalists and academics do not the whole country's intelligentsia make. Malaysia is full of well-educated people still, and what they now need to do is to consider the Malaysian Spring as an incredible chance to redevelop a culture of healthy, intelligent and dispassionate discussion and debate.

First off, let's bring our present ceaseless commenting on blogs and on WhatsApp, Instagram and Facebook, out in the open. Let's organise debates and give a face to all the opinions we now express in the shadow of cyberspace.

To me, the important thing about expressing opinions openly is that you will have to tweak them and polish them. That is part and parcel of becoming publicly articulate, psychologically accepting of constructive criticism, and likewise tactically efficient in offering criticism. In the process, we are emboldened and we become confident about our ideas and cognisant of what the creative intellectual process actually looks like and feels like.

Debates can become a cultured affair and a central part of Malaysian culture, where the idea is not to win points but to have one's ideas mutually polished and one's ability to say what one thinks as concisely and precisely as possible. We should not have to pussyfoot around our diversity if we are embracing of it.

Secondly, let us all help raise the standard of journalism in this country through contributions as writers and essayists on the one hand, and through putting higher demands on journalistic writing in the country on the other.

Finally, let's make our universities a place where young minds are brave enough to express ideas even when they may be half-baked and honest enough to acknowledge that they are half-baked. That is all par for the course. Nothing gets properly baked without being half-baked along the way.

Literacy and articulatory skills, like charity, start at home. So the making of a new Malaysia requires that each citizen realise that the change has to start with him or her, and with how he or she breaks out of the fears of the past. There are no more excuses.

55

The Layers of Historical Significance of GE14[*]

Whatever one's politics may be, one has to admit that the origins of the Federation of Malaysia are complicated and are overlaps of compromises made over time to define a middle ground that was democratic enough and yet centralised enough to be comfortably stable.

The middle ground that developed, however, came almost always to be defined in terms of racial balances, to the detriment of other parameters relevant to a modern economy, such as class tensions, urban-rural divides and various socio-economic gaps.

The defeat of the long-standing Barisan Nasional government and its almost immediate implosion on 9 May 2018, can in a way be described as the result of the Najib Razak administration's unwise rejection of the middle ground, which allowed for the coming together of forces opposed to it. With the Islamists pulling on one side and Pakatan Harapan gathering substantial numbers of rural voters over to its urban support base, UMNO and its long-ruling coalition were side-lined.

Now, one can see 9 May 2018 as a unique election in that sense, i.e. simply an aberration in a system that had for a long time been the established situation. But that would leave a lot of questions unanswered, foremost of which involves the reformist agenda that

---

[*] 'Revisiting national history and the significance of GE14', *The Edge*, Malaysia, 30 July 2018

the new government under Tun Dr Mahathir Mohamad is keen to champion, and to be seen to champion.

Revisiting National History

The significance of 9 May, to any historian interested in Malaysian politics, is in fact enormous, and in some ways warrants a revisit to the whole post-war period. As you, dear reader, would know, accounts of history are refined and defined by the historian's art of periodisation.

Apart from a news reporter description of the election as an aberration, one could for example consider 9 May to be the finale to a Tale of Three Elections stretching from 2008 when the BN lost five states to the opposition, to 2013 when it held its ground without winning back much of what had been lost, and ending with its calamitous fall in 2018. At one level, this would be a description of the triumph of the electoral strategising of the supporters of Anwar Ibrahim following their defeat in the 2004 election; and at another, the inability of UMNO to keep the middle ground after the failure of Abdullah's exaggerated claims at reform in the aftermath of Mahathir's retirement in 2003.

This leads us to the third periodisation – the Inter-Mahathir Era. For quite some time after 2003, Malaysian analyses were about what awaited the country following the exit of the Great Leader. Society's eagerness for reform which Abdullah Badawi captured to such good effect in 2004 provided him with a long honeymoon period which, when it finally ended, also ended his political career. Najib took over the reins of government, and did what he could to regain the middle ground. On realising on election night 2013 that this was beyond his capacity to do, he began allowing his party and his followers to veer as far to the right as they dared to go. Meanwhile, the scandals that had often followed him increased in number, culminating in the incomprehensibly daring kleptocratic money-laundering scandals which history will remember as the 1MBD fiasco.

After watching two prime ministers dismantle whatever it was he thought to be his legacy, Tun Dr Mahathir Mohamad decided to return to the fray, and it is an undeniable testimony to his strategic skills that he has now returned to lead the country again.

Fourthly, if we move the time scale back to 1998, when Mahathir sacked his deputy Anwar Ibrahim, then we may consider the 1998-2018 period as a study in how a reform movement actually overcame all odds to topple the system it considered corrupt and incorrigible. This is notwithstanding the queer condition that it managed to tip the scales in its favour only after Mahathir, the man it came into being to combat, became chairman of its political expression, the Pakatan Harapan—a strange twist of fate indeed.

As Mahathir and Anwar joined forces again, this time to topple the BN regime, one has to wonder if the sentiments in support of the *Bangsa Malaysia* (Vision 2020) agenda forwarded by Mahathir in 1990 had become intertwined with those championed by Anwar in 1998 after he refused to leave the political scene despite being sacked in September 1998. The differences between these two are largely not essential ones, and whatever policy direction the new government decides to adopt will draw inspiration from the major tenets of these two visions for a future Malaysia.

Indeed, with the recent appointment by Mahathir of Lim Guan Eng as finance minister, the country is reminded of the ludicrousness of the age-old unspoken policy begun in the early 1970s that this vital position should be a racially privileged position reserved for a member of the majority race. This affront to other communities in many ways symbolised the Malay agenda and the excesses that it could easily slide into. With Lim now taking over that important portfolio, a closing to this difficult period is signalled which many hope will be a complete one. The 2018 implosion of the Barisan Nasional that was formed in the early 1970s to restart democracy in a starkly limited form and some would say with the dice loaded to favour the party claiming to represent the interests of the majority, adds credence to this point of view.

Going further back in time, the enormity of what happened on 9 May 2018 also refocuses on the original ambitions and hopes of the founding fathers—and the founding generation—of the country, who clearly believed that once a proper balance was struck between the different ethnic groups, a trajectory for economic growth, harmonious inter-ethnic relations, and international prominence was possible, perhaps not despite the diversity of the new nation, but because of it.

The abovementioned list of approaches towards understanding Malaysia in light of the fall of Barisan Nasional would not be complete if one does not pay due attention to the fact that 1946-2018 marks the rise, rise, rise and fall of UMNO. No one doubts that if it is to rise again, it must rise on the back of a new coalition formed around whatever new shape the party itself manages to achieve in the coming months and years.

There can be no Malaysianist who can claim in any believable manner that he is not deeply curious about what internal reforms UMNO will undergo, and what types of collaboration with other parties it will enter into, in order to regain the middle ground that it discarded so facetiously in recent times.

About the Author

Dato' Dr OOI KEE BENG is the Executive Director of Penang Institute. He was the Deputy Director (2011–17) of Singapore's ISEAS – Yusof Ishak Institute, where he had been a fellow since 2004. Born and raised in Penang, he received his PhD in Sinology from Stockholm University, where he was attached for 22 years.

He received the Darjah Setia Pangkuan Negeri (DSPN, Order of the Defender of the State) award from the Governor of Penang in July 2017, which carries the title "Dato'".

He is the founder-editor of the popular magazine *Penang Monthly* (Penang Institute) and the policy briefs ISSUES (Penang Institute) and *ISEAS Perspective* (ISEAS, Singapore). He is also editor of *Trends in Southeast Asia* (ISEAS) and *Sojourn* (ISEAS), and a long-time columnist for *The Edge*, Malaysia.

His book, *The Reluctant Politician: Tun Dr Ismail and His Time* (2006), won the 'Award of Excellence for Best Writing Published in Book Form on Any Aspect of Asia (Non-Fiction)'. His *Continent, Coast, Ocean: Dynamics of Regionalism in Eastern Asia*, co-edited with Ding Choo Ming, was named 'Top Academic Work' in 2008 by the ASEAN Book Publishers Association (ABPA).

Some of his other noted works include *The Eurasian Core and Its Edges: Dialogues with Wang Gungwu on the History of the World; Young and Malay: Growing Up in Multicultural Malaysia; Yusof Ishak: A Man of Many Firsts; In Lieu of Ideology: An Intellectual Biography of Goh Keng Swee; Lim Kit Siang: Defying the Odds;* and *The Right to Differ: A Biographical Sketch of Lim Kit Siang*.

He lectured for several years in the 1990s at Stockholm University on 'History of China'; 'General Knowledge of China'; and 'Chinese Philosophy'. He was Lecturing Adjunct Associate Professor for the NUS Southeast Asian Studies Programme's MA Course, 'Country Studies: Malaysia'—Term 2 (2009, 2010 & 2011) and Lecturing Visiting Associate Professor at the Department of Public and Social Administration, City University of Hong Kong.

He was Sweden's representative to the First World Wushu Championships in Beijing in 1991, and to the European Wushu Championships in London in 1992 where he won the Silver Medal. His translations of Chinese war manuals such as *Sunzi's Art of War*, *Wuzi's Art of War* and *Weiliaozi's Art of War* are the first from Classical Chinese into Swedish. Some of these are used by the Stockholm Military Academy for officer training.

He is also a trained mediator and member of the Asian International Arbitration Centre (AIAC).

www.ingramcontent.com/pod-product-compliance
Lightning Source LLC
Chambersburg PA
CBHW071641280326
41928CB00068B/2151